KARL POPPER

Born in Vienna in 1902, Karl Popper was educated at the University of Vienna where he took his PhD in 1928. The year before Hitler invaded Austria, Popper left Vienna to take up a position at the University of New Zealand at Christchurch. In 1946 he was invited to teach at the London School of Economics, where he became Professor of Logic and Scientific Method. He was knighted in 1972, and became a Companion of Honour in 1982. He was a Fellow of the Royal Society and a Fellow of the British Academy, of the American Academy of Arts and Sciences, and of other national and international academies. Karl Popper died in September 1994.

Sir Karl Popper, one of the truly original and creative thinkers of our times, has been called the greatest philosopher of science this century. His influence on the methodology of science has been immense, in spite of a great number of misunderstandings and misrepresentations of his teaching, and in addition to his seminal work in the natural sciences, he was well known for his important contributions to political theory and sociology. His major publications are *The Logic of Scientific Discovery*, *The Open Society and its Enemies*, *The Poverty of Historicism*, *Conjectures and Refutations*, *Objective Knowledge*, *Realism and the Aim of Science*, *The Open Universe* and *Quantum Theory and the Schism in Physics*.

In memory of the countless men, women and children
of all creeds or nations or races
who fell victims to the fascist and communist belief in
Inexorable Laws of Historical Destiny.

KARL POPPER

THE POVERTY OF HISTORICISM

London and New York

First published in Great Britain in 1957
ARK Edition 1986
Reprinted 1989
Reprinted 1991, 1994, 1997 by Routledge
11 New Fetter Lane, London EC4P 4EE
29 West 35th Street, New York, NY 10001

Printed and bound in Great Britain
by Cox & Wyman Ltd, Reading, Berkshire

ISBN 0 415 06569 0

HISTORICAL NOTE

THE fundamental thesis of this book—that the belief in historical destiny is sheer superstition, and that there can be no prediction of the course of human history by scientific or any other rational methods—goes back to the winter of 1919–20. The main outline was completed by 1935; it was first read, in January or February 1936, as a paper entitled 'The Poverty of Historicism', at a private session in the house of my friend Alfred Braunthal in Brussels. At this meeting, a former student of mine made some important contributions to the discussion. It was Dr. Karl Hilferding, soon to fall a victim of the Gestapo and of the historicist superstitions of the Third Reich. There were also some other philosophers present. Shortly afterwards, I read a similar paper in Professor F. A. von Hayek's Seminar, at the London School of Economics. Publication was delayed by some years because my manuscript was rejected by the philosophical periodical to which it was submitted. It was first published, in three parts, in *Economica*, N.S., vol. XI, no. 42 and 43, 1944, and vol. XII, no. 46, 1945. Since then, an Italian translation (Milano, 1954) and a French translation (Paris, 1956) have appeared in book form. The text of the present edition has been revised, and some additions have been made.

PREFACE

I TRIED to show, in *The Poverty of Historicism*, that historicism is a poor method—a method which does not bear any fruit. But I did not actually refute historicism.

Since then, I have succeeded in giving a refutation of historicism: *I have shown that, for strictly logical reasons, it is impossible for us to predict the future course of history.*

The argument is contained in a paper, 'Indeterminism in Classical Physics and in Quantum Physics', which I published in 1950. But I am no longer satisfied with this paper. A more satisfactory treatment will be found in a chapter on Indeterminism which is part of the *Postscript: After Twenty Years* to my *Logic of Scientific Discovery*.

In order to inform the reader of these more recent results, I propose to give here, in a few words, an outline of this *refutation of historicism*. The argument may be summed up in five statements, as follows:

(1) The course of human history is strongly influenced by the growth of human knowledge. (The truth of this premise must be admitted even by those who see in our ideas, including our scientific ideas, merely the by-products of *material* developments of some kind or other.)

(2) We cannot predict, by rational or scientific methods, the future growth of our scientific

knowledge. (This assertion can be logically proved, by considerations which are sketched below.)

(3) We cannot, therefore, predict the future course of human history.

(4) This means that we must reject the possibility of a *theoretical history*; that is to say, of a historical social science that would correspond to *theoretical physics*. There can be no scientific theory of historical development serving as a basis for historical prediction.

(5) The fundamental aim of historicist methods (see sections 11 to 16 of this book) is therefore misconceived; and historicism collapses.

The argument does not, of course, refute the possibility of every kind of social prediction; on the contrary, it is perfectly compatible with the possibility of testing social theories—for example, economic theories —by way of predicting that certain developments will take place under certain conditions. It only refutes the possibility of predicting historical developments to the extent to which they may be influenced by the growth of our knowledge.

The decisive step in this argument is statement (2). I think that it is convincing in itself: *if there is such a thing as growing human knowledge, then we cannot anticipate today what we shall know only tomorrow*. This, I think, is sound reasoning, but it does not amount to a *logical proof* of the statement. The proof of (2), which I have given in the publications mentioned, is complicated; and I should not be surprised if simpler proofs could be found. My proof consists in showing that *no scientific predictor*—whether a human scientist or a calculating machine—*can possibly predict, by scientific methods, its own future results*. Attempts to do so can attain their result only after the event, when it is too late for a predic-

tion; they can attain their result only after the prediction has turned into a retrodiction.

This argument, being purely logical, applies to
scientific predictors of any complexity, including
'societies' of interacting predictors. But this means that
no society can predict, scientifically, its own future
states of knowledge.

My argument is somewhat formal, and it may therefore be suspected to be without any real significance,
even if its logical validity is granted.

I have, however, tried to show the significance of
the problem in two studies. In the later of these studies,
The Open Society and its Enemies, I have selected some
events from the history of historicist thought, in order
to illustrate its persistent and pernicious influence upon
the philosophy of society and of politics, from Heraclitus and Plato to Hegel and Marx. In the earlier of
these two studies, *The Poverty of Historicism*, now published for the first time in English in book form, I have
tried to show the significance of historicism as a fascinating intellectual structure. I have tried to analyse its
logic—often so subtle, so compelling and so deceptive
—and I have tried to argue that it suffers from an inherent and irreparable weakness.

K. R. P.

Penn, Buckinghamshire,
July 1957

Some of the most discerning reviewers of this book
were puzzled by its title. It was intended as an allusion
to the title of Marx's book *The Poverty of Philosophy*
which, in turn, was alluding to Proudhon's *Philosophy
of Poverty*.

K. R. P.

Penn, Buckinghamshire,
July 1959.

CONTENTS

ix

Contents

INTRODUCTION

SCIENTIFIC interest in social and political questions is hardly less old than scientific interest in cosmology and physics; and there were periods in antiquity (I have Plato's political theory in mind, and Aristotle's collection of constitutions) when the science of society might have seemed to have advanced further than the science of nature. But with Galileo and Newton, physics became successful beyond expectation, far surpassing all the other sciences; and since the time of Pasteur, the Galileo of biology, the biological sciences have been almost equally successful. But the social sciences do not as yet seem to have found their Galileo.

In these circumstances, students who work in one or another of the social sciences are greatly concerned with problems of method; and much of their discussion of these problems is conducted with an eye upon the methods of the more flourishing sciences, especially physics. It was, for instance, a conscious attempt to copy the experimental method of physics which led, in the generation of Wundt, to a reform in psychology; and since J. S. Mill, repeated attempts had been made to reform on somewhat similar lines the method of the social sciences. In the field of psychology, these reforms may have had some measure of success, despite a great many disappointments. But in the theoretical social sciences, outside economics, little else but dis-appointment has come from these attempts. When these failures were discussed, the question was soon raised whether the methods of physics were really applicable to the social sciences. Was it not perhaps the obstinate belief in their applicability that was responsible for the much-deplored state of these studies?

The query suggests a simple classification of the schools of thought interested in the methods of the less successful sciences. According to their views on the applicability of the methods of physics, we may classify these schools as *pro-naturalistic* or as *anti-naturalistic*; labelling them 'pro-naturalistic' or 'positive' if they favour the application of the methods of physics to the social sciences, and 'anti-naturalistic' or 'negative' if they oppose the use of these methods.

Whether a student of method upholds anti-natural-istic or pro-naturalistic doctrines, or whether he adopts a theory combining both kinds of doctrines, will largely depend on his views about the character of the science under consideration, and about the character of its subject-matter. But the attitude he adopts will also depend on his views about the methods of physics. I believe this latter point to be the most important of all. And I think that the crucial mistakes in most method-ological discussions arise from some very common misunderstandings of the methods of physics. In par-ticular, I think they arise from a misinterpretation of the logical form of its theories, of the methods of testing them, and of the logical function of observation and experiment. My contention is that these misunder-standings have serious consequences; and I will try to justify this contention in parts III and IV of this study. There I will try to show that various and sometimes conflicting arguments and doctrines, anti-naturalistic

2

as well as pro-naturalistic, are indeed based upon a misunderstanding of the methods of physics. In parts I and II, however, I will confine myself to the explanation of certain anti-naturalistic and pro-naturalistic doctrines that form part of a characteristic approach in which both kinds of doctrines are combined.

This approach which I propose first to explain, and only later to criticize, I call 'historicism'. It is often encountered in discussions on the method of the social sciences; and it is often used without critical reflection, or even taken for granted. What I mean by 'historicism' will be explained at length in this study. It will be enough if I say here that I mean by 'historicism' an approach to the social sciences which assumes that *historical prediction* is their principal aim, and which assumes that this aim is attainable by discovering the 'rhythms' or the 'patterns', the 'laws' or the 'trends' that underlie the evolution of history. Since I am convinced that such historicist doctrines of method are at bottom responsible for the unsatisfactory state of the theoretical social sciences (other than economic theory), my presentation of these doctrines is certainly not unbiased. But I have tried hard to make a case in favour of historicism in order to give point to my subsequent criticism. I have tried to present historicism as a well-considered and close-knit philosophy. And I have not hesitated to construct arguments in its support which have never, to my knowledge, been brought forward by historicists themselves. I hope that, in this way, I have succeeded in building up a position really worth attacking. In other words, I have tried to perfect a theory which has often been put forward, but perhaps never in a fully developed form. This is why I have deliberately chosen the somewhat unfamiliar label 'historicism'. By introducing it I hope I shall avoid merely verbal quibbles:

for nobody, I hope, will be tempted to question
whether any of the arguments here discussed really or
properly or essentially belong to historicism, or what
the word 'historicism' really or properly or essentially
means.

I

THE ANTI-NATURALISTIC
DOCTRINES OF HISTORICISM

IN strong opposition to methodological naturalism
in the field of sociology, historicism claims that some
of the characteristic methods of physics cannot be
applied to the social sciences, owing to the profound
differences between sociology and physics. Physical
laws, or the 'laws of nature', it tells us, are valid anywhere and always; for the physical world is ruled by
a system of physical uniformities invariable throughout space and time. Sociological laws, however, or the
laws of social life, differ in different places and periods.
Although historicism admits that there are plenty of
typical social conditions whose regular recurrence can
be observed, it denies that the regularities detectable
in social life have the character of the immutable
regularities of the physical world. For they depend
upon history, and upon differences in culture. They
depend on a particular *historical situation*. Thus one
should not, for example, speak without further qualification of the laws of economics, but only of the
economic laws of the feudal period, or of the early

industrial period, and so on; always mentioning the historical period in which the laws in question are assumed to have prevailed.

Historicism asserts that the historical relativity of social laws makes most of the methods of physics inapplicable to sociology. Typical historicist arguments on which this view is based concern generalization, experiment, the complexity of social phenomena, the difficulties of exact prediction, and the significance of methodological essentialism. I will treat these arguments in turn.

I   GENERALIZATION

The possibility of generalization and its success in the physical sciences rests, according to historicism, on the general uniformity of nature: upon the observation —perhaps better described as an assumption—that in similar circumstances similar things will happen. This principle, which is taken to be valid throughout space and time, is said to underlie the method of physics.

Historicism insists that this principle is necessarily useless in sociology. Similar circumstances only arise within a single historical period. They never persist from one period to another. Hence there is no long-run uniformity in society on which long-term generalizations could be based—that is, if we disregard *trivial regularities*, such as those described by the truism that human beings always live in groups, or that the supply of certain things is limited and the supply of others, like air, unlimited, and that only the former can have any market or exchange value.

A method which ignores this limitation and attempts a generalization of social uniformities will, according to historicism, implicitly assume that the regularities in question are everlasting; so that a methodologically naïve view—the view that the method of generalization can be taken over from physics by the social sciences—will produce a false and dangerously misleading sociological theory. It will be a theory denying that society develops; or that it ever changes significantly; or that social developments, if there are any, can affect the basic regularities of social life.

Historicists often emphasize that behind such mistaken theories there is usually an apologetic purpose; and indeed, the assumption of unchanging sociological laws can easily be misused for such ends. It may appear, first, as the argument that unpleasant or undesirable things must be accepted since they are determined by invariable laws of nature. For example, the 'inexorable laws' of economics have been invoked to demonstrate the futility of statutory interference with the wage bargain. A second apologetic misuse of the assumption of persistence is the fostering of a general feeling of inevitability, and thus of a readiness to endure the inevitable calmly and without protest. What is now will be for ever, and attempts to influence the march of events, or even to evaluate it, are ridiculous: one does not argue against the laws of nature, and attempts to overthrow them can only lead to disaster.

These, says the historicist, are the conservative, apologetic, and even fatalistic arguments which are the necessary corollaries of the demand that a naturalist method should be adopted in sociology.

The historicist opposes them by maintaining that social uniformities differ widely from those of the natural sciences. They change from one historical period to another, and *human* activity is the force that changes them. For social uniformities are not laws of nature, but man-made; and although they may be said to depend on human nature, they do so because

7

human nature has the power to alter and, perhaps, to control them. Therefore things can be bettered or worsened: active reform need not be futile.

These tendencies of historicism appeal to those who feel a call to be active; to interfere, especially with human affairs, refusing to accept the existing state of things as inevitable. The tendency towards activity and against complacency of any kind may be called '*activism*'. I will say more about the relations of historicism to activism in sections 17 and 18; but I may here quote the well-known exhortation of a famous historicist, Marx, which strikingly expresses the 'activist' attitude: 'The philosophers have only *interpreted* the world in various ways; the point however is to *change it.*'[1]

2   EXPERIMENT

Physics uses the method of experiment; that is, it introduces artificial controls, artificial isolation, and thereby ensures the reproduction of similar conditions, and the consequent production of certain effects. This method is obviously based on the idea that where circumstances are similar, similar things will happen. The historicist claims that this method is not applicable in sociology. Nor would it be useful, he argues, even if it were applicable. For, as similar conditions occur only within the limits of a single period, the outcome of any experiment would be of very limited significance. Moreover, artificial isolation would eliminate precisely those factors in sociology which are most important. Robinson Crusoe and his isolated individual economy can never be a valuable model of an economy whose problems arise precisely from the economic interaction of individuals and groups.

[1] See the eleventh of his *Theses on Feuerbach* (1845); see also section 17, below.

It is further argued that no really valuable experiments are possible. Large-scale experiments in sociology are never experiments in the physical sense. They are not made to advance knowledge as such, but to achieve political success. They are not performed in a laboratory detached from the outside world; rather, their very performance changes the conditions of society. They can never be repeated under precisely similar conditions since the conditions were changed by their first performance.

3   NOVELTY

The argument just mentioned deserves elaboration. Historicism, I have said, denies the possibility of repeating large-scale social experiments in precisely similar conditions, since the conditions of the second performance must be influenced by the fact that the experiment has been performed before. This argument rests on the idea that society, like an organism, possesses a sort of memory of what we usually call its history.

In biology, we can speak of the life-history of an organism since an organism is partially conditioned by past events. If such events are repeated, they lose, for the experiencing organism, their character of newness, and become tinged with habit. Yet this is precisely why the experience of the repeated event is *not* the same as the experience of the original event—why the experience of a repetition is *new*. Repetition of observed events can therefore correspond to the emergence of novel experiences in an observer. Since it forms new habits, repetition produces new, habitual conditions. The sum total of the conditions—internal and external—under which we repeat a certain experiment on one and the same organism cannot therefore be sufficiently similar for us to speak of a genuine repetition. For even an exact repetition of environmental conditions would be combined with new internal conditions in the organism: the organism learns by experience.

The same, according to historicism, holds true of society, since society too experiences: it too has its history. It may learn only slowly from the (partial) repetitions of its history, but it cannot be doubted that it does learn, in so far as it is partially conditioned by its past. Traditions and traditional loyalties and resentments, trust and distrust, could not otherwise play their important role in social life. Real repetition must therefore be impossible in social history; and this means that one must expect that events of an intrinsically new character will emerge. History may repeat itself—but never on the same level, especially if the events concerned are of historical importance, and if they exert a lasting influence on society.

In the world described by physics nothing can happen that is truly and intrinsically new. A new engine may be invented, but we can always analyse it as a re-arrangement of elements which are anything but new. Newness in physics is merely the newness of arrangements or combinations. In direct opposition to this, social newness, like biological newness, is an intrinsic sort of newness, historicism insists. It is real newness, irreducible to the novelty of arrangements. For in social life, the same old factors in a new arrangement are never really the same old factors. Where nothing can repeat itself precisely, real novelty must always be emerging. This is held to be significant for the consideration of the development of new stages or periods of history, each of which differs intrinsically from any other.

Historicism claims that nothing is of greater moment than the emergence of a really new period. This all-important aspect of social life cannot be investigated along the lines we are accustomed to follow when we explain novelties in the realm of physics by regarding them as re-arrangements of familiar elements. Even if the ordinary methods of physics were applicable to society, they would never be applicable to its most important features: *its division into periods, and the emergence of novelty.* Once we grasp the significance of social newness, we are forced to abandon the idea that the application of ordinary physical methods to the problems of sociology can aid us in understanding the problems of social development.

There is a further aspect of social newness. We have seen that every particular social happening, every single event in social life, can be said to be new, in a certain sense. It may be classified with other events; it may resemble those events in certain aspects; but it will always be unique in a very definite way. This leads, as far as sociological explanation is concerned, to a situation which is markedly different from that in physics. It is conceivable that, by analysing social life, we may be able to discover, and to understand intuitively, how and why any particular event came about; that we may clearly understand its *causes and effects*—the forces which occasioned it and its influence on other events. Yet we may nevertheless find that we are unable to formulate *general laws* which would serve as a description, in general terms, of such causal links. For it may be only the one particular sociological situation, and no other, which could be correctly explained by the particular forces that we have discovered. And these forces may well be unique: they may emerge only once, in this particular social situation, and never again.

4   COMPLEXITY

The methodological situation just sketched has a number of further aspects. One which has been discussed very frequently (and which will not be discussed here) is the sociological role of certain unique personalities. Another of these aspects is the complexity of social phenomena. In physics we are dealing with a subject-matter which is much less complicated; in spite of that, we further simplify matters artificially by the method of experimental isolation. Since this method is not applicable in sociology we are faced with a twofold complexity—a complexity arising out of the impossibility of artificial isolation, and a complexity due to the fact that social life is a natural phenomenon that presupposes the mental life of individuals, i.e. psychology, which in its turn presupposes biology, which again presupposes chemistry and physics. The fact that sociology comes last in this hierarchy of sciences plainly shows us the tremendous complexity of the factors involved in social life. Even if there were immutable sociological uniformities, like the uniformities in the field of physics, we might very well be unable to find them, owing to this twofold complexity. But if we cannot find them, then there is little point in maintaining that they nevertheless exist.

5   INEXACTITUDE OF PREDICTION

It will be shown in the discussion of its pro-naturalistic doctrines that historicism is inclined to stress the importance of prediction as one of the tasks of science. (In this respect, I quite agree with it, even though I do *not* believe that *historical prophecy* is one of the tasks of the social sciences.) Yet historicism argues that social prediction must be very difficult, not only on account of the complexity of social structures, but also on account of a peculiar complexity arising from the interconnection between predictions and the predicted events.

The idea that a prediction may have influence upon the predicted event is a very old one. Oedipus, in the legend, killed his father whom he had never seen before; and this was the direct result of the prophecy which had caused his father to abandon him. This is why I suggest the name '*Oedipus effect*' for the influence of the prediction upon the predicted event (or, more generally, for the influence of an item of information upon the situation to which the information refers), whether this influence tends to bring about the predicted event, or whether it tends to prevent it.

Historicists have recently pointed out that this kind of influence may be relevant to the social sciences; that it may increase the difficulty of making exact predictions and endanger their objectivity. They say that absurd consequences would follow from the assumption that the social sciences could ever be so far developed as to permit *precise* scientific forecasts of every kind of social fact and event, and that this assumption can therefore be refuted on purely logical grounds. For, if such a novel kind of scientific social calendar were constructed and became known (it could not be kept secret for long since it could in principle be re-discovered by anybody) it would certainly cause actions which would upset its predictions. Suppose, for instance, it were predicted that the price of shares would rise for three days and then fall. Plainly, everyone connected with the market would sell on the third day, causing a fall of prices on that day and falsifying the prediction. The idea, in short, of an exact and detailed calendar of social events is self-contradictory; and *exact and detailed* scientific social predictions are therefore impossible.

6 OBJECTIVITY AND VALUATION

In stressing the difficulties of prediction in the social sciences, historicism, we have seen, advances arguments which are based on an analysis of the influence of predictions upon predicted events. But according to historicism, this influence can, under certain circumstances, have important repercussions upon the predicting observer. Similar considerations play a part even in physics, where every observation is based on an exchange of energy between the observer and the observed; this leads to the uncertainty, usually negligible, of physical predictions, which is described by the 'principle of indeterminacy'. It is possible to maintain that this uncertainty is due to an interaction between the observed object and the observing subject since both belong to the same physical world of action and interaction. As Bohr has pointed out, there are analogies in other sciences to this situation in physics, especially in biology and psychology. But nowhere is the fact that the scientist and his object belong to the same world of greater moment than in the social sciences, where it leads (as has been shown) to an uncertainty of prediction, which is sometimes of great practical significance.

We are faced, in the social sciences, with a full and complicated interaction between observer and observed, between subject and object. The awareness of the existence of tendencies which might produce a future event, and, furthermore, the awareness that the prediction might itself exert an influence on events predicted is likely to have repercussions on the content of the prediction; and the repercussions might be of such a kind as gravely to impair the objectivity of the predictions and of other results of research in the social sciences.

A prediction is a social happening which may interact with other social happenings, and among them with the one which it predicts. It may, as we have seen, help to precipitate this event; but it is easy to see that it may also influence it in other ways. It may, in an extreme case, even *cause* the happening it predicts: the happening might not have occurred at all if it had not been predicted. At the other extreme the prediction of an impending event may lead to its *prevention* (so that, by deliberately or negligently abstaining from predicting it, the social scientist, it may be said, could bring it about, or could cause it to happen). There will clearly be many intermediate cases between these two extremes. The action of predicting something, and that of abstaining from prediction, might both have all sorts of consequences.

Now it is clear that social scientists must, in time, become aware of these possibilities. A social scientist may, for instance, predict something, foreseeing that his prediction will cause it to happen. Or he may deny that a certain event is to be expected, thereby preventing it. And in both cases he may be observing the principle which seems to ensure scientific objectivity: of telling the truth and nothing but the truth. But though he has told the truth, we cannot say that he has observed scientific objectivity; for in making forecasts (which forthcoming happenings fulfil) he may have influenced those happenings in the direction that he personally preferred.

The historicist may admit that this picture is somewhat schematic, but he will insist that it brings out sharply a point we find in almost every chapter of the social sciences. The interaction between the scientist's pronouncements and social life almost invariably creates situations in which we have not only to consider the truth of such pronouncements, but also their actual influence on future developments. The social scientist may be striving to find the truth; but, at the same time, he must always be exerting a definite influence upon society. The very fact that his pronouncements *do* exert an influence destroys their objectivity.

We have so far been assuming that the social scientist really strives to find the truth, and nothing but the truth; but the historicist will point out that the situation we have described brings out the difficulties of our assumption. For where predilections and interests have such influence on the content of scientific theories and predictions, it must become highly doubtful whether bias can be determined and avoided. Thus we need not be surprised to find that there is very little in the social sciences that resembles the objective and ideal quest for truth which we meet in physics. We must expect to find as many tendencies in the social sciences as can be found in social life; as many standpoints as there are interests. It may be questioned whether this historicist argument does not lead to that extreme form of relativism which holds that objectivity, and the ideal of truth, are altogether inapplicable in the social sciences where only success—political success—can be decisive.

To illustrate these arguments the historicist may point out that whenever there is a certain tendency inherent in a period of social development, we may expect to find sociological theories which influence this development. Social science may thus function as a midwife, helping to bring forth new social periods; but it can equally well serve, in the hands of conservative interests, to retard impending social changes.

Such a view may suggest the possibility of analysing and explaining the differences between the various sociological doctrines and schools, by referring either to their connection with the predilections and interests prevailing in a particular historical period (an approach which has sometimes been called 'historism', and should not be confused with what I call 'historicism'), or to their connection with political or economic or class interests (an approach which has sometimes been called the '*sociology of knowledge*').

7   HOLISM

Most historicists believe that there is an even deeper reason why the methods of physical science cannot be applied to the social sciences. They argue that sociology, like all 'biological' sciences, i.e. all sciences that deal with living objects, should not proceed in an atomistic, but in what is now called a 'holistic' manner. For the objects of sociology, social groups, must never be regarded as mere aggregates of persons. The social group is *more* than the mere sum total of its members, and it is also *more* than the mere sum total of the merely personal relationships existing at any moment between any of its members. This is readily seen even in a simple group consisting of three members. A group founded by A and B will be different in character from a group consisting of the same members but founded by B and C. This may illustrate what is meant by saying that a group has a *history* of its own, and that its structure depends to a great extent on its history (see also section 3 above on 'Novelty'). A group can easily retain its character intact if it loses some of its less important members. And it is even conceivable that a group may keep much of its original character even if *all* of its original members are replaced by others.

But the same members who now constitute the group might possibly have built up a very different group, if they had not entered the original group one by one, but founded a new one instead. The personalities of its members may have a great influence on the history and structure of the group, but this fact does not prevent the group from having a history and a structure of its own; nor does it prevent the group from strongly influencing the personalities of its members.

All social groups have their own traditions, their own institutions, their own rites. Historicism claims that we must study the history of the group, its traditions and institutions, if we wish to understand and explain it as it is now, and if we wish to understand and perhaps to foresee, its future development.

The holistic character of social groups, the fact that such groups are never fully explained as mere aggregates of their members, throws light on the historicist's distinction between novelty in physics, which merely involves new combinations or arrangements of elements and factors which themselves are not new, and novelty in social life, which is real and irreducible to a mere novelty of arrangement. For if social structures in general cannot be explained as combinations of their parts or members, then clearly it must be impossible to explain *new* social structures by this method.

Physical structures, on the other hand, can be explained as mere 'constellations', historicism insists, or as the mere sum of their parts, together with their geometrical configuration. Take the solar system, for instance; although it may be interesting to study its history, and although this study may throw light on its present state, we know that, in a sense, this state is independent of the history of the system. The structure of the system, its future movements and developments, are fully determined by the present constellation of its members. Given the relative positions, masses, and momenta, of its members at any one instant, the future movements of the system are all fully determined. We do not require additional knowledge as to which of the planets is older, or which was brought into the system from outside: the history of the structure, although it may be interesting, contributes nothing to our understanding of its behaviour, of its mechanism, and of its future development. It is obvious that a physical structure differs widely in this respect from any social structure; the latter cannot be understood, nor its future predicted, without a careful study of its history, even if we had complete knowledge of its momentary 'constellation'.

Such considerations strongly suggest that there is a close connection between historicism and the so-called *biological or organic theory* of social structures—the theory which interprets social groups by analogy with living organisms. Indeed, holism is said to be characteristic of biological phenomena in general, and the holistic approach is regarded as indispensable in considering how the history of various organisms influences their behaviour. The holistic arguments of historicism are thus apt to stress the similarity between social groups and organisms, although they need not necessarily lead to an acceptance of the biological theory of social structures. Similarly, the well-known theory of the existence of a *group-spirit*, as the carrier of the *group-traditions*, although not necessarily itself a part of the historicist argument, is closely related to the holistic view.

8   INTUITIVE UNDERSTANDING

We have dealt so far mainly with certain characteristic aspects of social life, such as novelty, complexity, organicity, holism, and the way its history falls into periods; aspects which, according to historicism, render certain typical methods of physics inapplicable to the social sciences. A more historical method of approach is therefore considered necessary in social studies. It is part of the anti-naturalistic view of historicism that we must try to understand intuitively the history of the various social groups, and this view is sometimes developed into a methodological doctrine which is very closely related to historicism, although it is not invariably combined with it.

It is the doctrine that the proper method of the social sciences, as opposed to the method of the natural sciences, is based upon an intimate understanding of social phenomena. The following oppositions and contrasts are usually stressed in connection with this doctrine. Physics aims at causal explanation: sociology at an understanding of purpose and meaning. In physics events are explained rigorously and quantitatively, and with the aid of mathematical formulae. Sociology tries to understand historical developments in more qualitative terms, for example, in terms of conflicting tendencies and aims, or in terms of 'national character', or 'spirit of the age'. This is why physics operates with inductive generalizations whereas sociology can only operate with the help of sympathetic imagination. And it is also the reason why physics can arrive at universally valid uniformities, and explain particular events as instances of such uniformities, whereas sociology must be content with the intuitive understanding of unique events, and of the role they play in particular situations, occurring within particular struggles of interests, tendencies, and destinies.

I propose to distinguish between three different variants of the doctrine of intuitive understanding. The first asserts that a social event is understood when analysed in terms of the forces that brought it about, i.e. when the individuals and groups involved, their purposes or interests, and the power they can dispose of, are known. The actions of individuals or groups are here understood as being in accordance with their aims—as promoting their real advantage or, at least, their imagined advantage. The method of sociology is here thought of as an imaginative reconstruction of either rational or irrational activities, directed towards certain ends.

The second variant goes further. It admits that such an analysis is necessary, particularly in regard to the understanding of individual actions or group activities. But it maintains that more is needed for the understanding of social life. If we want to understand the meaning of a social event, a certain political action for instance, then it is not enough to understand, teleologically, how and why it was brought about. Over and above that, we must understand its meaning, the significance of its occurrence. What is here meant by 'meaning' and 'significance'? From the standpoint I am describing as the second variant, the reply would be: a social event not only exerts certain influences, it not only leads, in time, to other events, but its very coming into existence changes the situational value of a wide range of other events. It creates a new situation, demanding a re-orientation and re-interpretation of all objects and of all actions in that particular field. To understand such an event as, say, the creation of a new army in a certain country, it is necessary to analyse intentions, interests, and so forth. But we cannot fully understand the meaning or significance of this action without also analysing its situational value; the military forces of another country, for example, which were fully sufficient for its protection up to that time, may now have become quite inadequate. In short, the

whole *social situation* may have changed, even before
any further factual changes have occurred, either
physical or even psychological; for the situation may
have changed long before the change has been noticed
by anybody. Thus in order to understand social life,
we must go beyond the mere analysis of factual causes
and effects, i.e. of motives, interests, and reactions
caused by actions: we have to understand every event
as playing a certain characteristic part within the
whole. The event gains its significance from its influence upon the whole, and its significance is therefore
in part determined by the whole.

The third variant of the doctrine of intuitive understanding goes even further, while fully admitting
everything maintained by the first and second variant.
It holds that to understand the meaning or significance
of a social event, more is required than an analysis of
its genesis, effects, and situational value. Over and
above such an analysis, it is necessary to analyse objective, underlying historical trends and tendencies
(such as the growth or decline of certain traditions or
powers) prevailing at the period in question, and to
analyse the contribution of the event in question to the
historical process by which such trends become manifest. A full understanding of the Dreyfus Affair, for
instance, demands over and above an analysis of its
genesis, effects, and situational value, an insight into
the fact that it was the manifestation of the contest
between two historical tendencies in the development
of the French Republic, democratic and autocratic,
progressive and reactionary.

This third variant of the method of intuitive understanding, with its emphasis on historical trends or
tendencies, is a position which suggests to a certain
extent the application of *inference by analogy* from one
historical period to another. For though it fully recog-

nizes that historical periods are intrinsically different, and that no event can really repeat itself in another period of social development, it can admit that analogous tendencies may become dominant in different periods which are, perhaps, very far removed from one another. Such similarities or analogies have been said to hold, for instance, between Greece before Alexander, and Southern Germany before Bismarck. The method of intuitive understanding suggests, in such cases, that we should evaluate the meaning of certain events by comparing them with analogous events in earlier periods, so as to help us to forecast new developments —never forgetting, however, that the inevitable differences between the two periods must be duly taken into account.

We see, accordingly, that a method capable of understanding the meaning of social events must go far beyond causal explanation. It must be holistic in character; it must aim at determining the role played by the event within a complex structure—within a whole which comprises not only contemporaneous parts but also the successive stages of a temporal development. This may explain why the third variant of the method of intuitive understanding tends to rely upon the analogy between an organism and a group, and why it tends to operate with ideas such as that of a mind or spirit of an age, the source and overseer of all those historical tendencies or trends which play such an important role in determining the meaning of sociological events.

But the method of intuitive understanding does not only fit in with the ideas of holism. It also agrees very well with the historicist's emphasis on novelty; for novelty cannot be causally or rationally explained, but only intuitively grasped. It will be seen, furthermore, in the discussion of the pro-naturalistic doctrines of historicism, that there is a very close connection be-tween them and our 'third variant' of the method of intuitive understanding, with its emphasis on historical tendencies or 'trends'. (See, for example, section 16.)

9   QUANTITATIVE METHODS

Among the oppositions and contrasts usually stressed in connection with the doctrine of intuitive under-standing the following has frequently been emphasized by historicists. In physics, it is said, events are ex-plained rigorously and precisely, in quantitative terms, and with the aid of mathematical formulae. Sociology, on the other hand, tries to understand historical de-velopment more in qualitative terms; for example, in terms of conflicting tendencies and aims.

The argument against the applicability of quanti-tative and mathematical methods is by no means peculiar to historicists; and, indeed, such methods are sometimes repudiated even by writers with strong anti-historicist views. But some of the most persuasive arguments against quantitative and mathematical methods bring out very well the point of view which I call historicism, and these arguments will be dis-cussed here.

When we consider the opposition to the use of quantitative and mathematical methods in sociology, a strong objection must at once occur to us: this attitude seems to be in conflict with the facts that quantitative and mathematical methods are actually being used with great success in some of the social sciences. How, in face of this, can it be denied that they are applicable?

Against this objection, the opposition to the quanti-tative and mathematical point of view may be upheld by some arguments characteristic of historicist ways of thinking.

I quite agree, the historicist may say, with your remarks; but there still remains a tremendous difference between the statistical methods of the social sciences and the quantitative-mathematical methods of physics. The social sciences know nothing that can be compared to the *mathematically formulated causal laws of physics*.

Consider, for instance, the physical law that (for light of any given wave-length) the smaller the aperture through which a light ray passes, the greater is the angle of diffraction. A physical law of this type has the form: 'Under certain conditions, if magnitude A varies in a certain manner, then magnitude B also varies in some predictable manner'. In other words, such a law expresses a dependence of one measurable quantity on another and the manner in which the one quantity depends on the other is laid down in exact quantitative terms. Physics has been successful in expressing all its laws in this form. In order to achieve this, its first task was to translate all physical qualities into quantitative terms. For instance, it had to replace the qualitative description of a certain kind of light— e.g. a bright yellow-greenish light—by a quantitative description: light of a certain wave-length and of a certain intensity. Such a process of quantitatively describing physical qualities is obviously a necessary pre-requisite for the quantitative formulation of causal physical laws. These enable us to explain why something has happened; for example, under the assumption of the law concerning the relations between the width of an aperture and the angle of diffraction, we can give a causal explanation of an increase of the angle of diffraction in terms of the fact that the aperture was decreased.

Causal explanation, the historicist maintains, must also be attempted by the social sciences. They may, for instance, undertake to explain imperialism in terms of industrial expansion. But if we consider this example we see at once that it is hopeless to attempt to express sociological laws in quantitative terms. For if we consider some such formulation as 'the tendency towards territorial expansion increases with the intensity of industrialization' (a formulation which at least is an intelligible, though probably *not* a true description of facts) we shall very soon find that we lack any method which could measure the tendency towards expansion, or the intensity of industrialization.

To sum up the historicist argument against quantitative-mathematical methods, it is the sociologist's task to give a causal explanation of the changes undergone, in the course of history, by such social entities as, for instance, states, or economic systems, or forms of government. As there is no known way of expressing in quantitative terms the qualities of these entities, no quantitative laws can be formulated. Thus, the causal laws of the social sciences, supposing that there are any, must differ widely in character from those of physics, being qualitative rather than quantitative and mathematical. If sociological laws determine the degree of anything, they will do so only in very vague terms, and will permit, at the best, a very rough scaling.

It appears that qualities—whether physical or nonphysical—can only be appraised by intuition. The arguments we have discussed here can therefore be used to support those that have been offered in favour of the method of intuitive understanding.

10 ESSENTIALISM *versus* NOMINALISM

The emphasis on the qualitative character of social events leads further to the problem of the status of the terms which denote qualities: to the so-called *problem*

of universals, one of the oldest and most fundamental
problems of philosophy.

This problem, over which a major battle raged
during the Middle Ages, is rooted in the philosophies of
Plato and Aristotle. It is usually interpreted as a
purely metaphysical problem; but like most metaphysical problems it can be re-formulated so as to become a problem of scientific method. We shall deal only
with the methodological problem here, giving a brief
outline of the metaphysical issue by way of an
introduction.

Every science uses terms which are called universal
terms, such as 'energy', 'velocity', 'carbon', 'whiteness', 'evolution', 'justice', 'state', 'humanity'. These
are distinct from the sort of terms which we call
singular terms or individual concepts, like 'Alexander
the Great', 'Halley's Comet', 'The First World War'.
Such terms as these are proper names, labels attached
by convention to the individual things denoted by
them.

Over the nature of universal terms a long and sometimes bitter dispute raged between two parties. One
held that universals differ from proper names only in
being attached to the members of a *set* or *class* of single
things, rather than to just one single thing. The universal term 'white', for instance, seemed to this party
to be nothing but a label attached to a set of many
different things—snowflakes, tablecloths, and swans, for
instance. This is the doctrine of the *nominalist* party. It
is opposed by a doctrine traditionally called *'realism'*—
a somewhat misleading name, as seen by the fact that
this 'realist' theory has also been called 'idealist'.
I therefore propose to re-name this anti-nominalistic
theory *'essentialism'*. Essentialists deny that we first
collect a group of single things and then label them
'white'; rather, they say, we call each single white

27

thing 'white' on account of a certain intrinsic property that it shares with other white things, namely 'whiteness'. This property, denoted by the universal term, is regarded as an object which deserves investigation just as much as the individual things themselves. (The name 'realism' derives from the assertion that universal objects, for instance, whiteness, 'really' exist, over and above single things and sets or groups of single things.) Thus universal terms are held to denote universal objects, just as singular terms denote individual things. These universal objects (called by Plato 'Forms' or 'Ideas') which are designated by the universal terms were also called 'essences'.

But essentialism not only believes in the existence of universals (i.e. of universal objects), it also stresses their importance for science. Singular objects, it points out, show many accidental features, features which are of no interest to science. To take an example from the social sciences: economics interests itself in money and credit, but it does not care about the particular shapes in which coins, banknotes or cheques appear. Science must strip away the accidental and penetrate to the essence of things. But the essence of anything is always something universal.

These last remarks indicate some of the methodological implications of this metaphysical problem. However, the methodological issue I am now going to discuss may in fact be considered independently of the metaphysical issue. We will approach it along another path—one that avoids the question of the existence of universal and singular objects, and of their differences. We will discuss merely the ends and means of science.

The school of thinkers whom I propose to call *methodological essentialists* was founded by Aristotle, who taught that scientific research must penetrate to the essence of things in order to explain them.

Methodological essentialists are inclined to formulate scientific questions in such terms as 'what is matter?' or 'what is force?' or 'what is justice?' and they believe that a penetrating answer to such questions, revealing the real or essential meaning of these terms and thereby the real or true nature of the essences denoted by them, is at least a necessary prerequisite of scientific research, if not its main task. *Methodological nominalists*, as opposed to this, would put their problems in such terms as 'how does this piece of matter behave?' or 'how does it move in the presence of other bodies?' For methodological nominalists hold that the task of science is only to describe how things behave, and suggest that this is to be done by freely introducing new terms wherever necessary, or by re-defining old terms wherever convenient while cheerfully neglecting their original meaning. For they regard *words* merely as *useful instruments of description.*

Most people will admit that methodological nominalism has been victorious in the natural sciences. Physics does not inquire, for instance, into the essence of atoms or of light, but it uses these terms with great freedom to explain and describe certain physical observations, and also as names of certain important and complicated physical structures. So it is with biology. Philosophers may demand from biologists the solution of such problems as 'what is life?' or 'what is evolution?' and at times some biologists may feel inclined to meet such demands. Nevertheless, scientific biology deals on the whole with different problems, and adopts explanatory and descriptive methods very similar to those used in physics.

Thus in the social sciences we should expect methodological naturalists to favour nominalism, and anti-naturalists to favour essentialism. Yet in fact essentialism seems to have the upper hand here; and it is not even faced by any very energetic opposition. It has therefore been suggested that *while the methods of the natural sciences are fundamentally nominalistic, social science must adopt a methodological essentialism.*[1] It is argued that the task of social science is to understand and explain such sociological entities as the state, economic action, the social group, etc., and that this can be done only by penetrating into their essences. Every important sociological entity presupposes universal terms for its description and it would be pointless freely to introduce new terms, as has been done so successfully in the natural sciences. The task of social science is to describe such entities clearly and properly, i.e. to distinguish the essential from the accidental; but this requires knowledge of their essence. Problems such as 'what is the State?' and 'what is a citizen?' (considered by Aristotle to be the basic problems of his *Politics*), or 'what is credit?' or 'what is the essential difference between the churchman and the sectarian (or the church and the sect)?' are not only perfectly legitimate, but are precisely the kind of question which sociological theories are designed to answer.

Although historicists may differ in their attitude towards the metaphysical issue, and in their opinion with regard to the methodology of natural science, it is clear that they will be inclined to side with essentialism and against nominalism so far as the methodology of social science is concerned. In fact, nearly every historicist I know of takes this attitude. But it is worth considering whether it is only the general anti-naturalistic tendency of historicism that accounts for this, or whether there are any specific historicist arguments that may be urged in favour of methodological essentialism.

[1] See section vi of ch. 3 of my *Open Society and Its Enemies*, especially note 30, and section ii of chapter 11.

In the first place it is clear that the argument against the use of quantitative methods in social science is relevant to this issue. The emphasis on the qualitative character of social events, together with the emphasis on intuitive understanding (as opposed to mere description), indicates an attitude closely related to essentialism.

But there are other arguments, more typical of historicism, which follow a trend of thought that will by now be familiar to the reader. (Incidentally, they are practically the same arguments as those which, according to Aristotle, led Plato to develop the first theory of essences.)

Historicism stresses the importance of change. Now in every change, the historicist might argue, there must be something that changes. Even if nothing remains unchanged, we must be able to identify what has changed in order to speak of change at all. This is comparatively easy in physics. In mechanics, for example, all changes are movements, i.e. spatio-temporal changes, of physical bodies. But sociology, which is chiefly interested in social institutions, faces greater difficulties, for such institutions are not so easy to identify after they have undergone change. In the simple descriptive sense it is not possible to regard a social institution *before* a change as the same as that institution *after* a change; it might, from the descriptive point of view, be entirely different. A naturalistic description of contemporary institutions of government in Britain, for example, might have to present them as entirely different from what they were four centuries ago. Yet we can say that, in so far as there is a *government*, it is *essentially* the same, even although it may have changed considerably. Its function within modern society is *essentially* analogous to the function it then fulfilled. Though hardly any describable features have remained the same, the *essential* identity of the

31

institution is preserved, permitting us to regard one institution as a changed form of the other: we cannot speak, in the social sciences, of changes or developments without presupposing an unchanging essence, and hence without proceeding in accordance with methodological essentialism.

It is plain, of course, that some sociological terms, such as depression, inflation, deflation, etc., were originally introduced in a purely nominalistic fashion. But even so they have not retained their nominalistic character. As conditions change, we soon find social scientists disagreeing about whether certain phenomena are really inflations or not; thus for the sake of precision it may become necessary to investigate the essential nature (or the essential meaning) of inflation.

So it can be said of any social entity that it 'might, so far as its *essence* is concerned, be present at any other place and in any other form, and might likewise change whilst remaining in fact unchanged, or change otherwise than in the way in which it actually does' (Husserl). The extent of possible changes cannot be limited *a priori*. It is impossible to say what sort of change a social entity can withstand and yet remain the same. Phenomena which from some standpoints may be essentially different, may from others be essentially the same.

From the historicist arguments developed above, it follows that a bare description of social developments is impossible; or rather, that a sociological description can never be merely a description in the nominalist sense. And if a sociological description cannot dispense with essences, a theory of social development will be even less able to do so. For who would deny that problems such as the determination and explanation of the characteristic features of a certain social period, together with its tensions and intrinsic tendencies and trends, must defy all attempts at treatment by nominalist methods?

Methodological essentialism can accordingly be based on the historicist argument which actually led Plato to his metaphysical essentialism, the Heraclitean argument that changing things defy rational description. Hence science or knowledge presupposes something that does not change but remains identical with itself—an essence. *History*, i.e. the description of change, and *essence*, i.e. that which remains unchanged during change, appear here as correlative concepts. But this correlation has yet another side: in a certain sense, an essence also presupposes change, and thereby history. For if that principle of a thing which remains identical or unchanged when the thing changes is its essence (or idea, or form, or nature, or substance), then the changes which the thing undergoes bring to light different sides or aspects or possibilities of the thing and therefore of its essence. The essence, accordingly, can be interpreted as the sum or source of the potentialities inherent in the thing, and the changes (or movements) can be interpreted as the realization or actualization of the hidden potentialities of its essence. (This theory is due to Aristotle.) It follows that a thing, i.e. its unchanging essence, can be known only *through its changes*. If, for instance, we want to find out whether a certain thing is made of gold, we have to beat it, or to test it chemically, thus changing it and thereby unfolding some of its hidden potentialities. In the same way, the essence of a man—his personality— can only be known as it unfolds itself in his biography. Applying this principle to sociology we are led to the conclusion that the essence or the real character, of a social group can reveal itself, and be known, only through its history. But if social groups can be known only through their history, the concepts used to describe them must be historical concepts; and indeed, such sociological concepts as the Japanese *state* or the Italian *nation* or the Aryan *race* can hardly be interpreted as anything but concepts based on the study of history. The same is valid for social *classes*: the *bourgeoisie*, for instance, can only be defined by its history: as the class that came to power through the industrial revolution, that pushed aside the landlords, and that is fighting and being fought by the proletariat, etc.

Essentialism may have been introduced on the ground that it enables us to detect an identity in things that change, but it furnishes in its turn some of the most powerful arguments in support of the doctrine that the social sciences must adopt a historical method; that is to say, in support of the doctrine of historicism.

II

THE PRO-NATURALISTIC
DOCTRINES OF HISTORICISM

ALTHOUGH historicism is fundamentally anti-naturalistic, it is by no means opposed to the idea that there is a common element in the methods of the physical and the social sciences. This may be due to the fact that historicists as a rule adopt the view (which I fully share) that sociology, like physics, is a branch of knowledge which aims, at the same time, to be *theoretical* and *empirical*.

By saying that it is a *theoretical* discipline we mean that sociology has to *explain and to predict* events, with the help of theories or of universal laws (which it tries to discover). By describing sociology as *empirical*, we mean to say that it is backed by experience, that the events it explains and predicts are *observable* facts, and that *observation* is the basis for the acceptance or rejection of any propounded theory. When we speak of success in physics we have in mind the success of its predictions: and the success of its predictions can be said to be the same as the empirical corroboration of the laws of physics. When we contrast the relative success of sociology with the success of physics, then we are assuming that success in sociology would likewise consist, basically, in the corroboration of predictions. It follows that certain methods—prediction with the help of laws, and the testing of laws by observation—must be common to physics and sociology.

I fully agree with this view, in spite of the fact that I consider it one of the basic assumptions of historicism. But I do not agree with the more detailed development of this view which leads to a number of ideas which I shall describe in what follows. At first sight these ideas might appear to be fairly straightforward consequences of the general view just outlined. But in fact, they involve other assumptions, namely, the antinaturalistic doctrines of historicism; and more especially, the doctrine of *historical laws or trends*.

11   COMPARISON WITH ASTRONOMY.
LONG-TERM FORECASTS AND
LARGE-SCALE FORECASTS[1]

Modern historicists have been greatly impressed by the success of Newtonian theory, and especially by its power of forecasting the position of the planets a long time ahead. The possibility of such *long-term forecasts*, they claim, is thereby established, showing that the old dreams of prophesying the distant future do not transcend the limits of what may be attained by the human mind. The social sciences must aim just as high. *If it is possible for astronomy to predict eclipses, why should it not be possible for sociology to predict revolutions?*

Yet though we ought to aim so high, we should never forget, the historicist will insist, that the social sciences cannot hope, and that they must not try, to attain the

---

[1] The first two paragraphs of this section are now inserted to replace a longer passage omitted in 1944 because of the paper shortage.

precision of astronomical forecasts. An exact scientific calendar of social events, comparable to, say, the Nautical Almanack, has been shown (in sections 5 and 6) to be logically impossible. Even though revolutions may be predicted by the social sciences, no such prediction can be exact; there must be a margin of uncertainty as to its details and as to its timing.

While conceding, and even emphasizing, the deficiencies of sociological predictions with respect to detail and precision, historicists hold that the sweep and the significance of such forecasts might compensate for these drawbacks. The deficiencies arise mainly from the complexity of social events, from their interconnections, and from the qualitative character of sociological terms. But although social science in consequence suffers from vagueness, its qualitative terms at the same time provide it with a certain richness and comprehensiveness of meaning. Examples of such terms are 'culture clash', 'prosperity', 'solidarity', 'urbanization', 'utility'. Predictions of the kind described, i.e. long-term predictions whose vagueness is balanced by their scope and significance, I propose to call *'predictions on a large scale'* or *'large-scale forecasts'*. According to historicism, this is the kind of prediction which sociology has to attempt.

It is certainly true that such large-scale forecasts—long-term forecasts of a wide range and possibly somewhat vague—can be achieved in some sciences. Instances of important and fairly successful large-scale prediction can be found within the field of astronomy. Examples are the prediction of sun-spot activity on the basis of periodic laws (significant for climatic variations) or of daily and seasonal changes in the ionization of the upper atmosphere (significant for wireless communication). These resemble eclipse predictions in so far as they deal with events in a comparatively distant future, but they differ from them in being often merely statistical and in any case less exact with respect to details, timing, and other features. We see that large-scale predictions are not perhaps impracticable in themselves; and if long-term forecasts are at all attainable by the social sciences then it is fairly clear that they can only be what we have described as large-scale forecasts. On the other hand, it follows from our exposition of the anti-naturalistic doctrines of historicism that *short-term predictions* in the social sciences must suffer from great disadvantages. Lack of exactness must affect them considerably, for by their very nature they can deal only with details, with the smaller features of social life, since they are confined to brief periods. But a prediction of details which is inexact in its details is pretty useless. Thus, if we are at all interested in social predictions, large-scale forecasts (which are also long-term forecasts) remain, according to historicism, not only the most fascinating but actually the only forecasts worth attempting.

12   THE OBSERVATIONAL BASIS

A non-experimental observational basis for a science is, in a certain sense of the term, always 'historical' in character. That is so even with the observational basis of astronomy. The facts on which astronomy is based are contained in the records of the observatory; records which inform us, for instance, that at such and such a date (hour, second) the planet Mercury has been observed by Mr. So-and-so in a certain position. In short, they give us a 'register of events in order of time', or a chronicle of observations.

Similarly, the observational basis of sociology can be given only in the form of a chronicle of events, namely of political or social happenings. This chronicle of political and other important happenings in social life is what one customarily calls 'history'. History in this narrow sense is the basis of sociology.

It would be ridiculous to deny the importance of history in this narrow sense as an empirical basis for social science. But one of the characteristic claims of historicism which is closely associated with its denial of the applicability of the experimental method, is that history, political and social, is the *only* empirical source of sociology. Thus the historicist visualizes sociology as a theoretical and empirical discipline whose empirical basis is formed by a chronicle of the facts of history alone, and whose aim is to make forecasts, preferably large-scale forecasts. Clearly, *these forecasts must also be of a historical character*, since their testing by experience, their verification or refutation, must be left to future history. Thus the making and testing of large-scale historical forecasts is the task of sociology as seen by historicism. In brief, the historicist claims that *sociology is theoretical history*.

13   SOCIAL DYNAMICS

The analogy between social science and astronomy can be developed further. The part of astronomy which historicists usually consider, celestial mechanics, is based on dynamics, the theory of motions as determined by forces. Historicist writers have often insisted that sociology should be based in a similar way on a social dynamics, the theory of social movement as determined by social (or historical) forces.

Statics, the physicist knows, is only an abstraction from dynamics; it is, as it were, the theory of how and why, under certain circumstances, nothing happens, i.e. why change does not occur; and it explains this by the equality of counteracting forces. Dynamics, on the other hand, deals with the general case, i.e. with forces equal or unequal, and might be described as the theory of how and why something does happen. Thus, only dynamics can give us the real, universally valid laws of mechanics; for nature is process; it moves, changes, develops—although sometimes only slowly, so that some developments may be difficult to observe.

The analogy of this view of dynamics to the historicist's view of sociology is obvious and needs no further comment. But, the historicist might claim, the analogy goes deeper. He might claim, for instance, that sociology, as conceived by historicism, is akin to dynamics because it is essentially a causal theory; for causal explanation in general is an explanation of how and why certain things happened. Basically, such an explanation must always have an historical element. If you ask someone who has broken his leg how and why it happened, you expect that he will tell you the history of the accident. But even on the level of theoretical thought, and especially on the level of theories permitting prediction, a historical analysis of the causes of an event is necessary. A typical example of the need for a historical causal analysis, the historicist will assert, is the problem of the origins, or the essential causes, of war.

In physics, such an analysis is achieved by a determination of the interacting forces, i.e. by dynamics; and the historicist claims that the same should be attempted by sociology. It has to analyse the forces which produce social change and create human history. From dynamics we learn how the interacting forces constitute new forces; and conversely, by analysing forces into their components, we are able to penetrate into the more fundamental causes of the events under consideration. Similarly, historicism demands the recognition of the fundamental importance of historical forces, whether spiritual or material; for example, religious or ethical ideas, or economic interests. To analyse, to disentangle this thicket of conflicting tendencies and forces and to penetrate to its roots, to the universal driving forces and laws of social change —this is the task of the social sciences, as seen by historicism. Only in this way can we develop a theoretical science on which to base those large-scale forecasts whose confirmation would mean the success of social theory.

14   HISTORICAL LAWS

We have seen that sociology, to the historicist, is theoretical history. Its scientific forecasts must be based on laws, and since they are historical forecasts, forecasts of social change, they must be based on historical laws.

But at the same time the historicist holds that the method of generalization is inapplicable to social science, and that we must not assume uniformities of social life to be invariably valid through space and time, since they usually apply only to a certain cultural or historical period. Thus social laws—if there are any real social laws—must have a somewhat different structure from the ordinary generalizations based on uniformities. Real social laws would have to be 'generally' valid. But this can only mean that they apply to the whole of human history, covering all of its periods rather than merely some of them. But there can be no social uniformities which hold good beyond single periods. Thus the only universally valid laws of society must be the laws which *link up the successive periods*. They must be *laws of historical development* which determine the transition from one period to another. This is what historicists mean by saying that the only real laws of sociology are historical laws.

15   HISTORICAL PROPHECY *versus*
      SOCIAL ENGINEERING

As indicated, these historical laws (if they can be discovered) would permit the prediction of even very
distant events, although not with minute exactness of
detail. Thus the doctrine that real sociological laws are
historical laws (a doctrine mainly derived from the
limited validity of social uniformities) leads back, independently of any attempt to emulate astronomy, to the
idea of 'large-scale forecasts'. And it makes this idea
more concrete, for it shows that these forecasts have
the character of historical prophecies.

Sociology thus becomes, to the historicist, an attempt
to solve the old problem of foretelling the future; not so
much the future of the individual as that of groups,
and of the human race. It is the science of things to
come, of impending developments. If the attempt to
furnish us with political foresight of scientific validity
were to succeed, then sociology would prove to be of
the greatest value to politicians, especially to those
whose vision extends beyond the exigencies of the
present, to politicians with a sense of historic destiny.
Some historicists, it is true, are content to predict only
the next stages of the human pilgrimage, and even
these in very cautious terms. But one idea is common
to them all—that sociological study should help to
reveal the political future, and that it could thereby
become the foremost instrument of far-sighted practical
politics.

From the point of view of the pragmatic value of
science, the significance of scientific predictions is clear
enough. It has not always been realized, however, that
two different kinds of prediction can be distinguished
in science, and accordingly two different ways of being

practical. We may predict (*a*) the coming of a typhoon, a prediction which may be of the greatest practical value because it may enable people to take shelter in time; but we may also predict (*b*) that if a certain shelter is to stand up to a typhoon, it must be constructed in a certain way, for instance, with ferroconcrete buttresses on its north side.

These two kinds of predictions are obviously very different although both are important and fulfil age-old dreams. In the one case we are told about an event which we can do nothing to prevent. I shall call such a prediction a '*prophecy*'. Its practical value lies in our being warned of the predicted event, so that we can side-step it or meet it prepared (possibly with the help of predictions of the other kind).

Opposed to these are predictions of the second kind which we can describe as *technological* predictions since predictions of this kind form a basis of *engineering*. They are, so to speak, constructive, intimating the steps open to us *if* we want to achieve certain results. The greater part of physics (nearly the whole of it apart from astronomy and meteorology) makes predictions of such a form that, considered from a practical standpoint, they can be described as technological prediction. The distinction between these two sorts of prediction roughly coincides with the lesser or greater importance of the part played by designed experiment, as opposed to mere patient observation, in the science concerned. The typical experimental sciences are capable of making technological predictions, while those employing mainly non-experimental observations produce prophecies.

I do not wish to be taken as implying that all sciences, or even all scientific predictions, are fundamentally practical—that they are necessarily either prophetic or technological and cannot be anything else. I only want to draw attention to a distinction between the two kinds of prediction and the sciences corresponding to them. In choosing the terms 'prophetic' and 'technological', I certainly wish to hint at a feature they exhibit if looked at from the pragmatic standpoint; but my use of this terminology is neither intended to mean that the pragmatic point of view is necessarily superior to any other, nor that scientific interest is limited to pragmatically important prophecies and to predictions of a technological character. If we consider astronomy, for example, then we have to admit that its findings are mainly of theoretical interest even though they are not valueless from a pragmatic point of view; but as 'prophecies' they are all akin to those of meteorology whose value for practical activities is quite obvious.

It is worth noting that this difference between the prophetic and the engineering character of sciences does not correspond to the difference between long-term and short-term predictions. Although most engineering predictions are short-term there are also long-term technological predictions, for instance, about the lifetime of an engine. Again, astronomical prophecies may be either short-term or long-term, and most meteorological prophecies are comparatively short-term.

The difference between these two practical aims—prophesying and engineering—and the corresponding difference in the structure of relevant scientific theories, will be seen later to be one of the major points in our methodological analysis. For the moment I only wish to stress that historicists, quite consistently with their belief that sociological experiments are useless and impossible, argue for historical prophecy—the prophecy of social, political and institutional developments—and against social engineering, as the practical aim of the social sciences. The idea of social engineering, the planning and construction of institutions, with the aim, perhaps, of arresting or of controlling or of quickening impending social developments, appears to some historicists as possible. To others, this would seem an almost impossible undertaking, or one which overlooks the fact that political planning, like all social activity, must stand under the superior sway of historical forces.

16   THE THEORY OF HISTORICAL DEVELOPMENT

These considerations have taken us to the very heart of the body of arguments which I propose to call 'historicism', and they justify the choice of this label. Social science is nothing but history: this is the thesis. Not, however, history in the traditional sense of a mere chronicle of historical facts. The kind of history with which historicists wish to identify sociology looks not only backwards to the past but also forwards to the future. It is the study of the operative forces and, above all, of the laws of social development. Accordingly, it could be described as historical theory, or as theoretical history, since the only universally valid social laws have been identified as historical laws. They must be laws of process, of change, of development—not the pseudo-laws of apparent constancies or uniformities. According to historicists, sociologists must try to get a general idea of the *broad trends* in accordance with which social structures change. But besides this, they should try to understand the causes of this process, the working of the forces responsible for change. They should try to formulate hypotheses about general trends underlying social development, in order that men may adjust themselves to impending changes by deducing prophecies from these laws.

The historicist's notion of sociology can be further clarified by following up the distinction I have drawn between the two different kinds of prognosis—and the related distinction between two classes of science. In opposition to the historicist methodology, we could conceive of a methodology which aims at a *technological social science*. Such a methodology would lead to the study of the general laws of social life with the aim of finding all those facts which would be indispensable as a basis for the work of everyone seeking to reform social institutions. There is no doubt that such facts exist. We know many Utopian systems, for instance, which are impracticable simply because they do not consider such facts sufficiently. The technological methodology we are considering would aim at furnishing means of avoiding such unrealistic constructions. It would be anti-historicist, but by no means anti-historical. Historical experience would serve it as a most important source of information. But, instead of trying to find laws of social development, it would look for the various laws which impose limitations upon the construction of social institutions, or for other uniformities (though these, the historicist says, do not exist).

As well as using counter-arguments of a kind already discussed, the historicist could question the possibility and the utility of such a social technology in another way. Let us assume, he could say, that a social engineer has worked out a plan for a new social structure, backed by the kind of sociology you have envisaged. This plan we suppose to be both practical and realistic in the sense that it does not conflict with the known facts and laws of social life; and we even assume that the plan is backed by an equally practicable further plan for transforming society as it is at present into the new structure. Even so, historicist arguments can show that such a plan would deserve no serious consideration. It would still remain an unrealistic and Utopian dream, just because it does not take account of the laws of historical development. Social revolutions are not brought about by rational plans, but by social forces, for instance, by conflicts of interests. The old idea of a powerful philosopher-king who would put into practice some carefully thought out plans was a fairy-tale invented in the interest of a land-owning aristocracy. The democratic equivalent of this fairy-tale is the superstition that enough people of good will may be persuaded by rational argument to take planned action. History shows that the social reality is quite different. The course of historical development is never shaped by theoretical constructions, however excellent, although such schemes might, admittedly, exert some influence, along with many other less rational (or even quite irrational) factors. Even if such a rational plan coincides with the interests of powerful groups it will never be realized in the way in which it was conceived, in spite of the fact that the struggle for its realization would then become a major factor in the historical process. The real outcome will always be very different from the rational construction. It will always be the resultant of the momentary constellation of contesting forces. Furthermore, under no circumstances could the outcome of rational planning become a stable structure; for the balance of forces is bound to change. All social engineering, no matter how much it prides itself on its realism and on its scientific character, is doomed to remain a Utopian dream.

So far, the historicist would continue, the argument has been directed against the practical possibility of social engineering backed by some theoretical social science, and not against the idea of such a science itself. It can easily be extended, however, so as to prove the impossibility of any theoretical social science of the technological kind. We have seen that practical engineering ventures must be doomed to failure on account of very important sociological facts and laws. But this implies not only that such a venture has no practical value but also that it is theoretically unsound, since it overlooks the only really important social laws—the laws of development. The 'science' upon which it was allegedly based must have missed these laws too, for otherwise it would never have furnished the basis for such unrealistic constructions. Any social science which does not teach the impossibility of rational social construction is entirely blind to the most important facts of social life, and must overlook the only social laws of real validity and of real importance. Social sciences seeking to provide a background for social engineering cannot, therefore, be true descriptions of social facts. They are impossible in themselves.

The historicist will claim that besides this decisive criticism there are other reasons for rejecting technological sociologies. One reason is, for example, that they neglect such aspects of the social development as the emergence of novelty. The idea that we can construct new social structures rationally on a scientific basis implies that we can bring into existence a new social period more or less precisely in the way we have planned it. Yet if the plan is based on a science that covers social facts, it cannot account for intrinsically new features, only for newness of arrangement (see section 3). But we know that a new period will have its own intrinsic novelty—an argument which must render any detailed planning futile, and any science upon which it is grounded untrue.

These historicist considerations can be applied to all social sciences, including economics. Economics, therefore, cannot give us any valuable information concerning social reform. Only a pseudo-economics can seek to offer a background for rational economic planning. Truly scientific economics can merely help to reveal the driving forces of economic development through different historical periods. It may help us to foresee the outlines of future periods, but it cannot help us to develop and put into operation any detailed plan for any new period. What holds for the other social sciences must hold for economics. Its ultimate aim can only be 'to lay bare the economic law of motion of human society' (Marx).

17   INTERPRETING *versus* PLANNING
SOCIAL CHANGE

The historicist view of social development does not imply fatalism nor need it lead to inactivity—quite the contrary. Most historicists have very marked tendencies towards 'activism' (see section 1). Historicism fully recognizes that our wishes and thoughts, our dreams and our reasoning, our fears and our knowledge, our interests and our energies, are all forces in the development of society. It does not teach that nothing can be brought about; it only predicts that neither your dreams nor what your reason constructs will ever be brought about *according to plan*. Only such plans as fit in with the main current of history can be effective. We can now see exactly the sort of activity admitted by historicists to be reasonable. Only such activities are reasonable as fit in with, and help along, the impending changes. Social midwifery is the only perfectly reasonable activity open to us, the only activity that can be based upon scientific foresight.

Although no scientific theory as such can directly encourage activity (it could only discourage certain activities as unrealistic), it can, by implication, give encouragement to those who feel that they ought to do something. Historicism definitely offers this kind of encouragement. It even gives human reason a certain part to play; for it is scientific reasoning, historicist social science, which alone can tell us the direction any reasonable activity must take if it is to coincide with the direction of impending changes.

Historical prophecy and the interpretation of history must thus become the basis of any thought-out and realistic social action. Consequently, interpretation of history must be the central job of historicist thought; and in point of fact it has become so. All the thoughts and all the activities of historicists aim at interpreting the past, in order to predict the future.

Can historicism offer hope or encouragement to those who want to see a better world? Only a historicist who takes an optimistic view of social development, believing it to be intrinsically 'good' or 'rational', in the sense of tending intrinsically towards a better, towards a more reasonable state of affairs, could offer such hope. But this view would amount to a belief in social and political miracles, since *it denies to human reason the power of bringing about a more reasonable world*. In fact, some influential historicist writers have optimistically foretold the coming of a realm of freedom, in which human affairs could be planned rationally. And they teach that the transition from the realm of necessity in which mankind at present suffers to the realm of freedom and reason cannot be brought about by reason but—miraculously—only by harsh necessity, by the blind and inexorable laws of historical development, to which they counsel us to submit.

Those who desire an increase in the influence of reason in social life can only be advised by historicism to study and interpret history, in order to discover the

laws of its development. If such interpretation reveals
that changes answering to their desire are impending,
then the desire is a reasonable one, for it agrees with
scientific prediction. If the impending development
happens to tend in another direction, then the wish to
make the world more reasonable turns out to be entirely unreasonable; to historicists it is then just a
Utopian dream. Activism can be justified only so long
as it acquiesces in impending changes and helps them
along.

I have already shown that the naturalistic method,
as seen by historicism, implies a definite sociological
theory—the theory that society does not significantly
develop or change. We now find that the historicist
method implies a strangely similar sociological theory
—the theory that society will necessarily change but
along a predetermined path that cannot change,
through stages predetermined by inexorable necessity.

'When a society has discovered the natural law that
determines its own movement, even then it can neither
overleap the natural phases of its evolution, nor shuffle
them out of the world by a stroke of the pen. But this
much it can do: it can shorten and lessen the birth-
pangs.' This formulation, due to Marx,[1] excellently
represents the historicist position. Although it teaches
neither inactivity nor real fatalism, historicism teaches
the futility of any attempt to alter impending changes;
a peculiar variety of fatalism, a fatalism in regard
to the trends of history, as it were. Admittedly, the
'activist' exhortation 'The philosophers have only *interpreted* the world in various ways: the point, however, is
to *change it*',[2] may find much sympathy with historicists (seeing that 'world' means here the developing

[1] Preface to *Capital*.
[2] This exhortation is also due to Marx (*Theses on Feuerbach*); see
above, end of section 1.

human society) because of its emphasis on change. But it is in conflict with the most significant doctrines of historicism. For as we now see, we may say: 'The historicist can only *interpret* social development and aid it in various ways; his point, however, is that *nobody can change it.*'

18   CONCLUSION OF THE ANALYSIS

It might be felt that my last formulations deviate from my avowed intention of outlining the historicist position as sharply and as convincingly as possible before proceeding to criticize it. For these formulations try to show that the leanings of some historicists towards optimism or activism are defeated by the outcome of the historicist analysis itself. This may seem to imply the charge that historicism is inconsistent. And it may be objected that it is not fair to allow criticism and irony to creep into an exposition.

I do not think this reproach would be just, however. Only those who are optimists or activists first, and historicists afterwards, can take my remarks as critical in an adverse sense. (There will be many who feel in this way: those who were originally attracted to historicism because of their leanings towards optimism or activism.) But to those who are primarily historicists, my remarks ought to appear not as a criticism of their historicist doctrines but only as a criticism of attempts to link it with optimism or activism.

Not all the forms of activism are thus criticized as incompatible with historicism, to be sure, but only some of its more extravagant forms. As compared with a naturalistic method, a pure historicist would argue, historicism does encourage activity, because of its stress on change, process, motion; yet it certainly cannot blindly countenance all kinds of activities as being reasonable from a scientific point of view; many possible activities are unrealistic, and their failure can be foreseen by science. This, he would say, is the reason why he and other historicists impose limitations on the scope of what they can admit to be useful activity, and why an emphasis upon these limitations is necessary for any clear analysis of historicism. And he might contend that the two Marxian quotations (in the foregoing section) do not contradict each other, but are complementary; that although the second (and older one) taken by itself could perhaps appear as slightly too 'activist', its proper limits are set by the first; and that should the second have appealed to over-radical activists and influenced them to embrace historicism, then the first ought to have taught them the proper limits of any activity, even though it may thereby have alienated their sympathies.

It seems to me for these reasons that my exposition is not unfair, but that it merely clears the ground in regard to activism. Similarly, I do not think that my other remark in the foregoing section, to the effect that historicist optimism must rest on faith alone (since reason is denied the role of bringing about a more reasonable world), is to be considered as an adverse criticism of historicism. It may appear adverse to those who are primarily optimists or rationalists. But the consistent historicist will see in this analysis only a useful warning against the romantic and Utopian character of both optimism and pessimism in their usual forms, and of rationalism too. He will insist that a truly scientific historicism must be independent of such elements; that we simply have to submit to the existing laws of development, just as we have to submit to the law of gravity.

The historicist may even go further. He may add that the most reasonable attitude to adopt is *so to adjust one's system of values as to make it conform with the impending changes.* If this is done, one arrives at a form of optimism which can be justified, since any change will then necessarily be a change for the better, if judged by that system of values.

Ideas of this kind have actually been held by some historicists, and have even been developed into a fairly coherent (and quite popular) historicist moral theory: the morally good is the morally progressive, i.e. the morally good is what is ahead of its time in conforming to such standards of conduct as will be adopted in the period to come.

This historicist moral theory, which could be described as 'moral modernism' or 'moral futurism' (it has its counterpart in an aesthetic modernism or futurism) accords well with the anti-conservative attitude of historicism; it can also be considered as a reply to certain questions concerning values (see section 6, on 'Objectivity and Valuation'). Above all, it can be looked upon as an indication that historicism—which, in this study, is seriously examined only in so far as it is a doctrine of method—might be amplified and developed into a full-scale philosophical system. Or, to put it in another way: it seems not improbable that the historicist method might have originated as a part of a general philosophical interpretation of the world. For there can be no doubt that, from the standpoint of history although not of logic, methodologies are usually by-products of philosophical views. I intend to examine these historicist philosophies elsewhere.[1] Here I will only criticize the methodological doctrines of historicism, as they were presented above.

[1] Since this was written, *The Open Society and Its Enemies* has been published. (London 1945; revised editions, Princeton 1950, London 1952, 1957; fourth edition, London 1961.) I was here alluding especially to ch. 22 of this book, entitled 'The Moral Theory of Historicism'.

III

CRITICISM OF
THE ANTI-NATURALISTIC
DOCTRINES

19   PRACTICAL AIMS OF THIS CRITICISM

WHETHER the true motive of scientific inquiry is the desire to know, that is to say, a purely theoretical or 'idle' curiosity, or whether we should rather understand science as an instrument for solving the practical problems that arise in the struggle for life, this is a question that need not be decided here. It will be admitted that the defenders of the rights of 'pure' or 'fundamental' research deserve every support in their fight against the narrow view, unfortunately again fashionable, that scientific research is justified only if it proves to be a sound investment.[1] But even the somewhat extreme view (to which

---

[1] The question is an old one. Even Plato sometimes attacks 'pure' research. For its defence, see T. H. Huxley, *Science and Culture* (1882), p. 19 f., and M. Polanyi, *Economica*, N.S., vol. VIII (1941), pp. 428 ff. (In addition to the books there quoted, see also Veblen, *The Place of Science in Modern Civilisation*, pp. 7 ff.)

I personally incline) that science is most significant as one of the greatest spiritual adventures that man has yet known may be combined with a recognition of the importance of practical problems and practical tests for the progress of science, whether applied or pure; for practice is invaluable for scientific speculation, both as a spur and as a bridle. One need not espouse pragmatism in order to appreciate Kant's saying: 'To yield to every whim of curiosity, and to allow our passion for inquiry to be restrained by nothing but the limits of our ability, this shows an eagerness of mind not unbecoming to *scholarship*. But it is *wisdom* that has the merit of selecting, from among the innumerable problems which present themselves, those whose solution is important to mankind.'[1]

The application of this to the biological and perhaps even more to the social sciences is clear. Pasteur's reform of the biological sciences was carried out under the stimulus of highly practical problems, which were in part industrial and agricultural. And social research nowadays has a practical urgency surpassing even that of cancer research. As Professor Hayek says, 'economic analysis has never been the product of detached intellectual curiosity about the *why* of social phenomena, but of an intense urge to reconstruct a world which gives rise to profound dissatisfaction';[2] and some of the social sciences, other than economics, that have not yet adopted this outlook, show by the barrenness of their results how urgently their speculations are in need of practical checks.

The need for the stimulus of practical problems is equally clear when we consider inquiries into the methods of scientific research, and more especially,

[1] Kant, *Dreams of a Ghost Seer*, part II, ch. III (*Werke*, ed. E. Cassirer, vol. II, p. 385).
[2] See *Economica*, vol. XIII (1933), p. 122.

into *the methods of the generalizing or theoretical social
sciences* with which we are concerned here. The more
fruitful debates on method are always inspired by certain practical problems which face the research worker;
and nearly all debates on method which are not so inspired are characterized by that atmosphere of futile
subtlety which has brought methodology into disrepute
with the practical research worker. It should be realized that methodological debates of the more practical
kind are not only useful but also necessary. In the development and improvement of method, as of science
itself, we learn only by trial and error, and we need the
criticism of others in order to find out our mistakes;
and this criticism is the more important since the introduction of new methods may mean a change of a
fundamental and revolutionary character. All this may
be illustrated by examples such as the introduction of
mathematical methods into economics, or of the so-
called 'subjective' or 'psychological' methods into
value theory. A more recent example is the combination of the methods of this theory with statistical
methods ('demand analysis'). This last revolution in
method was partly the outcome of prolonged and
largely critical debates; a fact from which the apologist
for the study of method may certainly draw encouragement.

A practical approach to the study of both the social
sciences and their method is advocated by many of the
followers of historicism who hope that they will be able
to transform, by the use of historicist methods, the
social sciences into a powerful instrument in the hands
of the politician. It is this recognition of the practical
task of the social sciences which provides something
like a common ground for discussion between the
historicists and some of their opponents; and I am
ready to take my own stand on this common ground

in order to criticize historicism as *a poor method*, unable to yield the results it promises.

20   THE TECHNOLOGICAL APPROACH
               TO SOCIOLOGY

Although in this study my topic is historicism, a doctrine of method with which I disagree, rather than those methods which, in my opinion, have been successful, and whose further and more conscious development I recommend, it will be useful to deal briefly with the successful methods first, so as to reveal to the reader my own bias and to clarify the point of view that underlies my criticism. For convenience, I shall label these methods '*piecemeal technology*'.

The term 'social technology' (and even more the term 'social engineering'[1] which will be introduced in the next section) is likely to arouse suspicion, and to repel those whom it reminds of the 'social blueprints' of the collectivist planners, or perhaps even of the 'technocrats'. I realize this danger, and so I have added the word 'piecemeal', both to off-set undesirable associations and to express my conviction that 'piecemeal tinkering' (as it is sometimes called), combined with critical analysis, is the main way to practical results in the social as well as in the natural sciences. The social sciences have developed very largely through the criticism of proposals for social improvements or, more precisely, through attempts to find out whether or not some particular economic or political action is likely to produce an expected, or desired, result.[2] This approach, which might indeed be called the classical

---

[1] For a defence of this term, see note 1 on p. 64, below.

[2] Cp. F. A. von Hayek, *Economica*, vol. XIII (1933), p. 123. ' . . . economics developed mainly as the outcome of the investigation and refutation of successive Utopian proposals . . .'

one, is what I have in mind when I refer to the technological approach to social science, or to 'piecemeal social technology'.

Technological problems in the field of social science may be of a 'private' or of a 'public' character. For example, investigations into the technique of business administration, or into the effects of improved working conditions upon output, belong to the first group. Investigations into the effects of prison reform or universal health insurance, or of the stabilization of prices by means of tribunals, or of the introduction of new import duties, etc., upon, say, the equalization of incomes, belong to the second group; and so do some of the most urgent practical questions of the day, such as the possibility of controlling trade cycles; or the question whether centralized 'planning', in the sense of state management of production, is compatible with an effective democratic control of the administration; or the question of how to export democracy to the Middle East.

This emphasis upon the practical technological approach does not mean that any of the theoretical problems that may arise from the analysis of the practical problems should be excluded. On the contrary, it is one of my main points that the technological approach is likely to prove fruitful in giving rise to significant problems of a purely theoretical kind. But besides helping us in the fundamental task of selecting problems, the technological approach imposes a discipline on our speculative inclinations (which, especially in the field of sociology proper, are liable to lead us into the region of metaphysics); for it forces us to submit our theories to definite standards, such as standards of clarity and practical testability. My point about the technological approach might perhaps be made by saying that sociology (and perhaps even the social sciences in general) should look, not indeed for 'its Newton or its Darwin'[1], but rather for its Galileo, or its Pasteur.

This and my previous references to an analogy between the methods of the social and the natural sciences are likely to provoke as much opposition as our choice of terms like 'social technology' and 'social engineering' (this in spite of the important qualification expressed by the word 'piecemeal'). So I had better say that I fully appreciate the importance of the fight against a dogmatic methodological naturalism or 'scientism' (to use Professor Hayek's term). Nevertheless I do not see why we should not make use of this analogy as far as it is fruitful, even though we recognize that it has been badly misused and misrepresented in certain quarters. Besides, we can hardly offer a stronger argument against these dogmatic naturalists than one that shows that some of the methods they attack are fundamentally the same as the methods used in the natural sciences.

A *prima facie* objection against what we call the technological approach is that it implies the adoption of an 'activist' attitude towards the social order (see section 1), and that it is therefore liable to prejudice us against the anti-interventionist or 'passivist' view: the view that if we are dissatisfied with existing social or economic conditions, it is because we do not understand how they work and why active intervention could only make matters worse. Now I must admit that I am certainly out of sympathy with this 'passivist' view, and that I even believe that a policy of *universal* anti-interventionism is untenable—even on

[1] See M. Ginsberg, in *Human Affairs* (ed. by R. B. Cattell and others), p. 180. It must be admitted, however, that the success of mathematical economics shows that one social science at least has gone through its Newtonian revolution.

purely logical grounds, since its supporters are bound
to recommend political intervention aimed at preventing intervention. Nevertheless, the technological
approach as such is neutral in this matter (as indeed
it ought to be), and by no means incompatible with
anti-interventionism. On the contrary, I think that anti-
interventionism involves a technological approach.
For to assert that interventionism makes matters worse
is to say that certain political actions would not have
certain effects—to wit, not the desired ones; and it is
one of the most characteristic tasks of any technology
to *point out what cannot be achieved*.

It is worth while to consider this point more closely.
As I have shown elsewhere,[1] every natural law can be
expressed by asserting that *such and such a thing cannot
happen*; that is to say, by a sentence in the form of the
proverb: 'You can't carry water in a sieve.' For example, the law of conservation of energy can be
expressed by: 'You cannot build a perpetual motion
machine'; and that of entropy by: 'You cannot build
a machine which is a hundred per cent efficient.' This
way of formulating natural laws is one which makes
their technological significance obvious and it may
therefore be called the '*technological form*' of a natural
law. If we now consider anti-interventionism in this
light, then we see at once that it may well be expressed
by sentences of the form: 'You cannot achieve such
and such results', or perhaps, 'You cannot achieve
such and such ends without such and such concomi-
tant effects.' But this shows that anti-interventionism
can be called a typically *technological doctrine*.

It is not, of course, the only one in the realm of social
science. On the contrary, the significance of our

[1] See my *Logic of Scientific Discovery* (1959), section 15. (Negated
existential propositions.) The theory may be contrasted with J. S. Mill,
Logic, Book V, ch. V, section 2.

analysis lies in the fact that it draws attention to a really fundamental similarity between the natural and the social sciences. I have in mind the existence of sociological laws or hypotheses which are analogous to the laws or hypotheses of the natural sciences. Since the existence of such sociological laws or hypotheses (other than so-called 'historical laws') has often been doubted,[1] I will now give a number of examples: 'You cannot introduce agricultural tariffs and at the same time reduce the cost of living.'—'You cannot, in an industrial society, organize consumers' pressure groups as effectively as you can organize certain producers' pressure groups.'—'You cannot have a centrally planned society with a price system that fulfils the main functions of competitive prices.'—'You cannot have full employment without inflation.' Another group of examples may be taken from the realm of power politics: 'You cannot introduce a political reform without causing some repercussions which are undesirable from the point of view of the ends aimed at' (therefore, look out for them).—'You cannot introduce a political reform without strengthening the opposing forces, to a degree roughly in ratio to the scope of the reform.' (This may be said to be the technological corollary of 'There are always interests connected with the *status quo*.')—'You cannot make a revolution without causing a reaction.' To these examples we may add two more, which may be called 'Plato's law of revolutions' (from the eighth book of the *Republic*) and 'Lord Acton's law of corruption', respectively: 'You cannot make a successful revolution if the ruling class is not weakened by internal dissension or defeat in war.'—'You cannot give a man power

---

[1] See, for example, M. R. Cohen, *Reason and Nature*, pp. 356 ff. The examples in the text appear to refute this particular anti-naturalistic view.

over other men without tempting him to misuse it—a temptation which roughly increases with the amount of power wielded, and which very few are capable of resisting.'[1] Nothing is here assumed about the strength of the available evidence in favour of these hypotheses whose formulations certainly leave much room for improvement. They are merely examples of the kind of statements which a piecemeal technology may attempt to discuss, and to substantiate.

[1] A similar formulation of this 'law of corruption' is discussed by C. J. Friedrich in his very interesting and partly technological *Constitutional Government and Politics* (1937). He says of this law that 'all the natural sciences cannot boast of a single "hypothesis" of equal importance to mankind' (p. 7). I do not doubt its importance; but I think that we may find countless laws of equal importance in the natural sciences, if only we look for them among the more platitudinous rather than among the more abstract laws. (Consider such laws as that men cannot live without food, or that vertebrates have two sexes.) Professor Friedrich insists upon the anti-naturalist thesis that the 'social sciences cannot benefit from applying the methods of the natural sciences to them' (*op. cit.*, p. 4). But he attempts, on the other hand, to base his theory of politics on a number of hypotheses of whose character the following passages (*op. cit.*, pp. 14 ff.) may give an idea: 'Consent and constraint are each a living force, generating power'; together, they determine 'the intensity of a political situation'; and since 'this intensity is determined by the absolute amount of either consent or constraint or both, it is perhaps most readily presented by the diagonal of the parallelogram of these two forces: consent and constraint. In that case its numerical value would equal the square root of the sum of the squares of the numerical values of consent and constraint'. This attempt to apply the Pythagorean theorem to a 'parallelogram' (we are not told why it should be rectangular) of 'forces' which are too vague to be measurable, seems to me an example not of anti-naturalism but of just that kind of naturalism or 'scientism' from which, I admit, the 'social sciences cannot benefit'. It may be noted that these 'hypotheses' can hardly be expressed in technological form, while the 'law of corruption', for example, whose importance is very justly emphasized by Friedrich, can be so expressed.

For the historical background of the 'scientistic' view that the problems of political theory can be understood in terms of the 'parallelogram of forces', see now my book, *The Open Society and Its Enemies* (revised edition), note 2 to ch. 7.

21   PIECEMEAL *versus* UTOPIAN
                    ENGINEERING

Notwithstanding the objectionable associations which
attach to the term 'engineering',[1] I shall use the term
'piecemeal social engineering' to describe the practical
application of the results of piecemeal technology. The
term is useful since there is need for a term covering
social activities, private as well as public, which, in
order to realize some aim or end, consciously utilize
all available technological knowledge.[2] Piecemeal
social engineering resembles physical engineering in
regarding the *ends* as beyond the province of technology. (All that technology may say about ends is
whether or not they are compatible with each other
or realizable.) In this it differs from historicism, which
regards the ends of human activities as dependent on
historical forces and so within its province.

Just as the main task of the physical engineer is to
design machines and to remodel and service them, the
task of the piecemeal social engineer is to design social

[1] Against the use of the term 'social engineering' (in the 'piecemeal'
sense) it has been objected by Professor Hayek that the typical engineering job involves the centralization of all relevant knowledge in a single
head, whereas it is typical of all truly social problems that knowledge has
to be used which cannot be so centralized. (See Hayek, *Collectivist Economic
Planning*, 1935, p. 210.) I admit that this fact is of fundamental importance. It can be formulated by the technological hypothesis: 'You
cannot centralize within a planning authority the knowledge relevant
for such tasks as the satisfaction of personal needs, or the utilization of
specialized skill and ability.' (A similar hypothesis may be proposed
regarding the impossibility of centralizing initiative in connection with
similar tasks.) The use of the term 'social engineering' may now be
defended by pointing out that the engineer must use the technological
knowledge embodied in these hypotheses which inform him of the limitations of his own intiative as well as of his own knowledge. See also note 1
on p. 90, below.

[2] Including, if it can be obtained, knowledge concerning the limitations of knowledge, as explained in the previous note.

64

institutions, and to reconstruct and run those already in existence. The term 'social institution' is used here in a very wide sense, to include bodies of a private as well as of a public character. Thus I shall use it to describe a business, whether it is a small shop or an insurance company, and likewise a school, or an 'educational system', or a police force, or a Church, or a law court. The piecemeal technologist or engineer recognizes that *only a minority of social institutions are consciously designed while the vast majority have just 'grown', as the undesigned results of human actions.*[1] But however strongly he may be impressed by this important fact, as a technologist or engineer he will look upon them from a 'functional' or 'instrumental' point of view.[2] He will see them as means to certain ends, or as convertible to the service of certain ends; as machines rather than as organisms. This does not mean, of course, that he will overlook the fundamental differences between institutions and physical instruments. On the contrary, the technologist should study the differences as well as the similarities, expressing his results in the form of hypotheses. And indeed, it is not difficult to formulate hypotheses about institutions

[1] The two views—that social institutions are either 'designed' or that they just 'grow'—correspond to those of the Social Contract theorists and of their critics, for example, Hume. But Hume does not give up the 'functional' or 'instrumentalist' view of social institutions, for he says that men could not do without them. This position might be elaborated into a Darwinian explanation of the instrumental character of un-designed institutions (such as language): if they have no useful function, they have no chance of surviving. According to this view, undesigned social institutions may emerge as *unintended consequences of rational actions*: just as a road may be formed without any intention to do so by people who find it convenient to use a track already existing (as Descartes observes). It need hardly be stressed, however, that the technological approach is quite independent of all questions of 'origin'.

[2] For the 'functional' approach, see B. Malinowski, for example, 'Anthropology as the Basis of Social Science', in *Human Affairs* (ed. Cattell), especially pp. 206 ff. and 239 ff.

in technological form as is shown by the following example: 'You cannot construct foolproof institutions, that is to say, institutions whose functioning does not very largely depend upon persons: institutions, at best, can reduce the uncertainty of the personal element, by assisting those who work for the aims for which the institutions are designed, and on whose personal initiative and knowledge success largely depends. (Institutions are like fortresses. They must be well designed *and* properly manned.)'[1]

The characteristic approach of the piecemeal engineer is this. Even though he may perhaps cherish some ideals which concern society 'as a whole'—its general welfare, perhaps—he does not believe in the method of re-designing it as a whole. Whatever his ends, he tries to achieve them by small adjustments and re-adjustments which can be continually improved upon. His ends may be of diverse kinds, for example, the accumulation of wealth or of power by certain individuals, or by certain groups; or the distribution of wealth and power; or the protection of certain 'rights' of individuals or groups, etc. Thus public or political social engineering may have the most diverse tendencies, totalitarian as well as liberal. (Examples of far-reaching liberal programmes for piecemeal reform

[1] This example, asserting that the efficiency of institutional 'machines' is limited, and that the functioning of institutions depends on their being supplied with proper personnel, may perhaps be compared with the principles of thermodynamics, such as the law of conservation of energy (in the form in which it excludes the possibility of a perpetual motion machine). As such, it may be contrasted with other 'scientistic' attempts to work out an analogy between the physical concept of energy and some sociological concepts such as power; see, for example, Bertrand Russell's *Power* (1938), p. 10 f., where this kind of scientistic attempt is made. I do not think that Russell's main point—that the various 'forms of power', such as wealth, propagandist power, naked power, may sometimes be 'converted' into one another—can be expressed in technological form.

have been given by W. Lippmann, under the title 'The Agenda of Liberalism'.[1]) The piecemeal engineer knows, like Socrates, how little he knows. He knows that we can learn only from our mistakes. Accordingly, he will make his way, step by step, carefully comparing the results expected with the results achieved, and always on the look-out for the unavoidable unwanted consequences of any reform; and he will avoid undertaking reforms of a complexity and scope which make it impossible for him to disentangle causes and effects, and to know what he is really doing.

Such 'piecemeal tinkering' does not agree with the political temperament of many 'activists'. Their programme, which too has been described as a programme of 'social engineering', may be called 'holistic' or 'Utopian engineering'.

Holistic or Utopian social engineering, as opposed to piecemeal social engineering, is never of a 'private' but always of a 'public' character. It aims at remodelling the 'whole of society' in accordance with a definite plan or blueprint; it aims at 'seizing the key positions'[2] and at extending 'the power of the State ... until the State becomes nearly identical with society',[3] and it aims, furthermore, at controlling from these 'key positions' the historical forces that mould the future of the developing society: either by arresting this development, or else by foreseeing its course and adjusting society to it.

[1] W. Lippmann, *The Good Society* (1937), ch. XI, pp. 203 ff. See also W. H. Hutt, *Plan for Reconstruction* (1943).

[2] The expression is often used by K. Mannheim in his *Man and Society in an Age of Reconstruction*; see his Index, and, for example, pp. 269, 295, 320, 381. This book is the most elaborate exposition of a holistic and historicist programme known to me and is therefore singled out here for criticism.

[3] See Mannheim, *ibid.*, 337. The passage is more fully quoted in section 23, where it is also criticized. (See note 2 on p. 79, below.)

It may be questioned, perhaps, whether the piece-meal and the holistic approaches here described are fundamentally different, considering that we have put no limits to the scope of a piecemeal approach. As this approach is understood here, constitutional reform, for example, falls well within its scope; nor shall I exclude the possibility that a series of piecemeal reforms might be inspired by one general tendency, for example, a tendency towards a greater equalization of incomes. In this way, piecemeal methods may lead to changes in what is usually called the 'class structure of society'. Is there any difference, it may be asked, between these more ambitious kinds of piecemeal engineering and the holistic or Utopian approach? And this question may become even more pertinent if we consider that, when trying to assess the likely consequences of some proposed reform, the piecemeal technologist must do his best to estimate the effects of any measure upon the 'whole' of society.

In answering this question, I shall not attempt to draw a precise line of demarcation between the two methods, but I shall try to bring out the very different point of view from which the holist and the piecemeal technologist look upon the task of reforming society. The holists reject the piecemeal approach as being too modest. Their rejection of it, however, does not quite square with their practice; for in practice they always fall back on a somewhat haphazard and clumsy although ambitious and ruthless application of what is essentially a piecemeal method without its cautious and self-critical character. The reason is that, in practice, the holistic method turns out to be impossible; the greater the holistic changes attempted, the greater are their unintended and largely unexpected repercussions, forcing upon the holistic engineer the expedient of piecemeal *improvization*. In fact, this

expedient is more characteristic of centralized or col-
lectivistic planning than of the more modest and careful piecemeal intervention; and it continually leads
the Utopian engineer to do things which he did not
intend to do; that is to say, it leads to the notorious
phenomenon of *unplanned planning*. Thus the difference
between Utopian and piecemeal engineering turns out,
in practice, to be a difference not so much in scale and
scope as in caution and in preparedness for unavoidable surprises. One could also say that, in practice,
the two *methods* differ in other ways than in scale and
scope—in opposition to what we are led to expect if
we compare the two *doctrines* concerning the proper
methods of rational social reform. Of these two doctrines, I hold that the one is true, while the other is
false and liable to lead to mistakes which are both
avoidable and grave. Of the two methods, I hold that
one is possible, while the other simply does not exist:
it is impossible.

One of the differences between the Utopian or
holistic approach and the piecemeal approach may
therefore be stated in this way: while the piecemeal
engineer can attack his problem with an open mind
as to the scope of the reform, the holist cannot do this;
for he has decided beforehand that a complete reconstruction is possible and necessary. This fact has far-
reaching consequences. It prejudices the Utopianist
against certain sociological hypotheses which state
limits to institutional control; for example, the one
mentioned above in this section, expressing the uncertainty due to the personal element, the 'human
factor'. By a rejection *a priori* of such hypotheses, the
Utopian approach violates the principles of scientific
method. On the other hand, problems connected with
the uncertainty of the human factor must force the
Utopianist, whether he likes it or not, to try to control

the human factor by institutional means, and to extend his programme so as to embrace not only the transformation of society, according to plan, but also the transformation of man.[1] 'The political problem, therefore, is to *organize human impulses* in such a way that they will direct their energy to the right strategic points, and steer the total process of development in the desired direction.' It seems to escape the well-meaning Utopianist that this programme implies an admission of failure, even before he launches it. For it substitutes for his demand that we build a new society, fit for men and women to live in, the demand that we 'mould' these men and women to fit into his new society. This, clearly, removes any possibility of testing the success or failure of the new society. For those who do not like living in it only admit thereby that they are not yet fit to live in it; that their 'human impulses' need further 'organizing'. But without the possibility of tests, any claim that a 'scientific' method is being employed evaporates. The holistic approach is incompatible with a truly scientific attitude.

Utopian engineering is not one of the main topics of this study, but there are two reasons why it will be considered in the next three sections, along with historicism. First, because under the name of collectivist (or centralized) planning, it is a very fashionable doctrine from which 'piecemeal technology' and 'piecemeal engineering' must be sharply distinguished. Secondly, because Utopianism not only resembles historicism in its hostility to the piecemeal approach, but also frequently joins forces with the historicist ideology.

[1] 'The Problem of Transforming Man' is the heading of a chapter of K. Mannheim's *Man and Society*. The following quotation is from that chapter, p. 199 f.

22   THE UNHOLY ALLIANCE WITH UTOPIANISM

That there is opposition between the two methodological approaches which I have called 'piecemeal
technology' and 'historicism' has been clearly recognized by Mill. 'There are two kinds of sociological
inquiry', he wrote.[1] 'In the first kind, the question proposed is, . . . for example, what would be the effect of
. . . introducing universal suffrage, in the present condition of society? . . . But there is also a second inquiry
. . . In this . . . the question is, not what will be the
effect of a given cause in a certain state of society, but
what are the causes which produce . . . States of Society
generally?' Considering that Mill's 'States of Society'
correspond precisely to what we have called 'historical periods', it is clear that his distinction between
the 'two kinds of sociological inquiry' corresponds
to our distinction between the approach of piecemeal technology and that of historicism; and this
becomes even more obvious if we follow more close'y
Mill's description of the 'second kind of sociological
inquiry' which (under the influence of Comte) he
declares to be superior to the first, and which he
describes as making use of what he calls 'the historical
method'.

As has been shown before (in sections 1, 17 and 18),
historicism is not opposed to 'activism'. A historicist
sociology can even be interpreted as a kind of technology which may help (as Marx puts it) to 'shorten and
lessen the birth pangs' of a new historical period. And
indeed, in Mill's description of the historical method
we can find this idea formulated in a manner which is

[1] See J. S. Mill, *Logic*, Book VI, ch. X, section 1.

strikingly similar to that of Marx:[1] 'The method now characterized is that by which . . . the laws . . . of social progress must be sought. By its aid we may here-after succeed not only in looking far forward into the future history of the human race, but in determining what artificial means may be used . . . to accelerate the natural progress in so far as it is beneficial . . . [2] Such practical instructions, founded on the highest branch of speculative sociology, will form the noblest and most beneficial portion of the Political Art.'

As indicated by this passage, it is not so much the fact that it is a technology as the fact that it is a *piece-meal* technology that marks the difference between my approach and that of the historicist. In so far as histori-cism is technological, its approach is not piecemeal, but 'holistic'.

Mill's approach is very clearly shown to be holistic when he explains what he means by a 'State of Society' (or historical period): 'What is called a state of society', he writes, '. . . is the simultaneous state of all the greater social facts or phenomena.' Examples of these facts are *inter alia*: 'The state of industry, of wealth and its distribution'; society's 'division into classes, and the relations of those classes to one an-other; the common beliefs which they entertain . . .; their form in government, and the more important of their laws and customs.' Summing up, Mill char-acterizes states of society as follows: 'States of society are like . . . different ages in the physical frame; they

[1] *Logic*, Book VI, ch. X, section 8. Marx's parallel passage (quoted above, in section 17) is taken from his preface to the first edition of *Capital*.

[2] This remark shows that Mill's Utilitarianism prevented him from defining 'beneficial' as synonymous with 'progressive'; that is to say, in spite of his progressivism, he did not uphold a historicist moral theory (cp. section 19) such as was developed by Spencer and Engels (and nowadays by C. H. Waddington; see his *Science and Ethics*).

are conditions not in one or a few organs or functions, but of *the whole organism*.'[1]

It is this holism which distinguishes historicism most radically from any piecemeal technology, and which makes possible its alliance with certain types of holistic or Utopian social engineering.

This is certainly a somewhat strange alliance; for as we have seen (in section 15) there is a very definite clash between the approach of the historicist and that of the social engineer or the technologist, provided we understand by social engineering the construction of social institutions according to plan. From the point of view of historicism, the historicist approach is just as radically opposed to any kind of social engineering as is the approach of a meteorologist to that of the magician who makes rain; accordingly, social engineering (even the piecemeal approach) has been attacked by historicists as Utopian.[2] In spite of that, we find historicism very frequently allied with just those ideas which are typical of holistic or Utopian social engineering, such as the idea of 'blueprints for a new order', or of 'centralized planning'.

Two characteristic representatives of this alliance are Plato and Marx. Plato, a pessimist, believed that all change—or almost all change—is decay; this was his law of historical development. Accordingly, his Utopian blueprint aims at arresting all change;[3] it is what would nowadays be called 'static'. Marx, on the other hand, was an optimist, and possibly (like Spencer) an adherent of a historicist moral theory. Accordingly, his Utopian blueprint was one of a developing or 'dynamic' rather than of an arrested society. He

[1] Mill, *ibid.*, section 2 (italics mine).
[2] See sections 15 to 17; see especially Engels' *Socialism, Utopian and Scientific*.
[3] I have discussed this at length in *The Open Society and Its Enemies*.

predicted, and tried actively to further, a development culminating in an ideal Utopia that knows no political or economic coercion: the state has withered away, each person co-operates freely in accordance with his abilities, and all his needs are satisfied.

The strongest element in the alliance between historicism and Utopianism is, undoubtedly, the holistic approach which is common to both. Historicism is interested in the development, not of aspects of social life, but of 'society as a whole'; and Utopian engineering is similarly holistic. Both overlook an important fact that will be established in the next section—the fact that 'wholes' in this sense can never be the object of scientific inquiry. Both parties are dissatisfied with 'piecemeal tinkering' and 'muddling through': they wish to adopt more radical methods. And both the historicist and the Utopianist seem to be impressed, and sometimes even deeply perturbed, by the experience of a changing social environment (an experience which is often frightening, and is sometimes described as a 'social breakdown'). Accordingly, they both attempt to rationalize this change, the one by prophesying the course of social development, and the other by insisting that the change should be strictly and completely controlled, or even that it should be entirely arrested. The control must be complete, for in any department of social life which is not so controlled, there may lurk the dangerous forces that make for unforeseen changes.

Another link between the historicist and the Utopianist is that both believe that their aims or ends are not a matter of choice, or of moral decision, but that they may be scientifically discovered by them within their fields of inquiry. (In this, they differ from the piecemeal technologist and engineer, just as much as from the physical engineer.) Both the historicist and the Utopianist believe that they can find out what the true aims or ends of 'society' are; for example, by determining its historical tendencies, or by diagnosing 'the needs of their time'. Thus they are apt to adopt some kind of historicist moral theory (see section 18). It is no accident that most authors who advocate Utopian 'planning' tell us that planning is simply inevitable, owing to the direction in which history is proceeding; and that we must plan, whether we like it or not.[1]

In the same historicist vein, these authors rebuke their opponents for being mentally backward, and believe that it is their main task 'to break the old habits of thought, and to find the new keys to the understanding of the changing world'.[2] They assert that trends of social change 'cannot be successfully influenced or even deflected' until we give up the piecemeal approach, or 'the spirit of "muddling through" '. But it may be doubted whether the new 'thought on the level of planning'[3] is as novel as it is supposed to be, since holism seems to have been characteristic of fairly

[1] See, for example, K. Mannheim's *Man and Society*, p. 6 (and many other places), where we are told that 'There is no longer any choice "between planning and not planning", but only a choice "between good planning and bad" '; or F. Zweig, *The Planning of Free Societies* (1942), p. 30, who answers the question whether a planned or an unplanned society is preferable by saying that this question does not arise, since it has been solved for us by the direction of the present historical development.

[2] K. Mannheim, *op. cit.*, p. 33; the next quotations are from *ibid.*, p. 7.

[3] K. Mannheim, not unlike Comte, distinguishes three 'levels' in the development of thought: (1) trial and error or chance discovery, (2) invention, (3) planning (*ibid.*, p. 150 f.). I am so far from agreeing with his doctrine that the trial and error method (1) appears to me to approach the method of science more closely than any of the other 'levels'.—An additional reason for considering the holistic approach to social science as pre-scientific is that it contains an element of perfectionism. Once we realize, however, that we cannot make heaven on earth but can only improve matters *a little*, we also realize that we can only improve them *little by little*.

75

ancient thought, from Plato onward. I personally believe that quite a good case may be made for the view that the holistic way of thinking (whether about 'society' or about 'nature'), so far from representing a high level or late stage in the development of thought, is characteristic of a pre-scientific stage.

23   CRITICISM OF HOLISM

Having revealed my own bias, and having sketched the point of view that underlies my criticism as well as the opposition between the piecemeal approach on the one hand and historicism and Utopianism on the other, I will now proceed to my main task, the examination of historicist doctrines. I begin with a brief criticism of holism, since this has now turned out to be one of the most crucial positions of the theory to be attacked.

There is a fundamental ambiguity in the use of the word 'whole' in recent holistic literature. It is used to denote (*a*) the totality of all the properties or aspects of a thing, and especially of all the relations holding between its constituent parts, and (*b*) certain special properties or aspects of the thing in question, namely those which make it appear an organized structure rather than a 'mere heap'. Wholes in sense (*b*) have been made the objects of scientific study, especially by the so-called '*Gestalt*' school of psychology; and there is indeed no reason why we should not study such aspects as the regularities of structure (for example, the symmetry) which can be found in certain things such as organisms, or electrical fields, or machines. Of things that possess such structures it may be said, as *Gestalt* theory puts it, that they are more than aggregates—'more than the mere sum of their parts'.

Any of the examples of *Gestalt* theory may be used to show that wholes in sense (*b*) are very different from wholes in sense (*a*). If, with the *Gestalt* theorists, we consider that a melody is more than a mere collection or sequence of single musical sounds, then it is *one of the aspects* of this sequence of sounds which we select for consideration. It is an aspect which may be clearly distinguished from other aspects, such as the absolute pitch of the first of these sounds, or their average absolute strength. And there are other *Gestalt* aspects which are even more abstract than those of melody, for example, the rhythm of the melody; for by considering rhythm we neglect even relative pitch, which is important for melody. By thus being selective, the study of a *Gestalt*, and with it, of any whole in sense (*b*), is sharply distinguished from the study of a totality, i.e. of a whole in sense (*a*).

The fact that wholes in sense (*b*) can be studied scientifically must therefore not be appealed to in order to justify the entirely different claim that wholes in sense (*a*) can be so studied. The latter claim must be rejected. If we wish to study a thing, we are bound to select certain aspects of it. It is not possible for us to observe or to describe a whole piece of the world, or a whole piece of nature; in fact, not even the smallest whole piece may be so described, since all description is necessarily selective.[1] It may even be said that wholes in sense (*a*) can never be the object of any activity, scientific or otherwise. If we take an organism and

[1] H. Gomperz, *Weltanschauungslehre*, II/I (1908), p. 63, points out that a piece of the world, such as a sparrow nervously fluttering about, may be described by the following widely different propositions, each corresponding to a different aspect of it: 'This bird is flying!'—'There goes a sparrow!'—'Look, here is an animal!'—'Something is moving here.'—'Energy is being transformed here.'—'This is not a case of perpetual motion.'—'The poor thing is frightened!' It is clear that it can never be the task of science to attempt the completion of such a list, which is necessarily infinite.—F. A. von Hayek, in *Ethics*, vol. LIV (1943), note 5, sketches a criticism of holism which is very similar to the one propounded here in the text.

transport it to another place, then we deal with it as a physical body, neglecting many of its other aspects. If we kill it, then we have destroyed certain of its properties, but never all of them. In fact, we cannot possibly destroy the totality of its properties and of all the inter-relations of its parts, even if we smash or burn it.

But the fact that wholes in the sense of totalities cannot be made the object of scientific study, or of any other activity such as control or reconstruction, seems to have escaped the holists, even those of them who admit that, as a rule, science is selective.[1] They do not doubt the possibility of a scientific grasp of social wholes (in the sense of totalities) because they rely on the precedent of *Gestalt* psychology. For they believe that the difference between the *Gestalt* approach and a treatment of social wholes in sense (*a*), embracing the 'structure of all social and historical events of an epoch', lies merely in the fact that a *Gestalt* may be grasped by direct intuitive perception, while social wholes are 'too intricate to be understood at a glance', so that they 'can only be gradually grasped after long thought, in which all elements are noted, compared, and combined'.[2] The holists do not see, in short, that *Gestalt* perception has simply nothing to do with wholes in sense (*a*), that all knowledge, whether intuitive or discursive, must be of abstract aspects, and that we can never grasp the 'concrete structure of social reality itself'.[3] Having overlooked this point,

[1] K. Mannheim describes (*op. cit.*, p. 167) selective or abstract science as 'a stage through which all sciences which strive for precision must pass'.

[2] With the following three quotations compare Mannheim, *op. cit.*, p. 184; see also p. 170, note, and p. 230.

[3] *Ibid.*, p. 230. The doctrine that we may obtain a kind of concrete knowledge of 'reality itself' is well known as a part of what can be technically described as *mysticism*; and so is the clamour for 'wholes'.

they insist that the specialist's study of 'petty details'
must be complemented by an 'integrating' or 'synthetic' method which aims at reconstructing 'the whole
process'; and they assert that 'sociology will continue
to ignore the essential question as long as specialists
refuse to see their problems as a whole'.[1] But this
holistic method necessarily remains a mere programme.
Not one example of a scientific description of a whole,
concrete social situation is ever cited. And it cannot
be cited, since in every such case it would always be
easy to point out aspects which have been neglected;
aspects that may nevertheless be most important in
some context or other.

Yet holists not only plan to study the whole society
by an impossible method, they also plan to control and
reconstruct our society 'as a whole'. They prophesy that
'the power of the State is bound to increase until the
State becomes nearly identical with society'.[2] The intuition expressed by this passage is clear enough. It is
the totalitarian intuition.[3] Yet what, apart from con-
veying this intuition, does the prophecy mean? The
term 'society' embraces, of course, all social relations,
including all personal ones; those of a mother to her
child as much as those of a child welfare officer to
either of the two. It is for many reasons quite impossible to control all, or 'nearly' all, these relationships;
if only because with every new control of social relations we create a host of new social relations to be

[1] See *op. cit.*, for example, pp. 26 and 32. My criticism of holism does
not mean that I am opposed to a plea for co-operation between the
various branches of science. Especially when we are faced with a definite
piecemeal problem which might be furthered by such co-operation,
nobody would dream of opposing it. But this is a very different matter
from the plan to grasp concrete wholes by a method of systematic
synthesis, or something of the sort.

[2] See *op. cit.*, p. 337; and note 3 on p. 67, above.

[3] The formula quoted is nearly identical with one by C. Schmitt.

controlled. In short, the impossibility is a logical impossibility.[1] (The attempt leads to an infinite regress;
the position is similar in the case of an attempt to
study the whole of society—which would have to include this study.) Yet there can be no doubt that
the Utopianists plan, precisely, to attempt the impossible; for they tell us that, among other things,
it will even be possible 'to mould personal inter-
course in a more realistic way'.[2] (Nobody doubts, of
course, that wholes in sense (*b*) can be moulded or
controlled or even created, as opposed to wholes in
sense (*a*); we can create a melody, for example; but
this has nothing to do with Utopian dreams of total
control.)

So much for Utopianism. As far as historicism is
concerned, the position is similarly hopeless. Historicist
holists often assert, by implication, that the historical
method is adequate for the treatment of wholes in the
sense of totalities.[3] But this assertion rests on a misunderstanding. It results from combining the correct
belief that history, as opposed to the theoretical
sciences, is interested in concrete individual events and
in individual personalities rather than in abstract
general laws, with the mistaken belief that the 'concrete' individuals in which history is interested can be
identified with 'concrete' wholes in sense (*a*). But they
cannot; for history, like any other kind of inquiry, can
only deal with selected aspects of the object in which

[1] Holists may hope that there is a way out of this difficulty by denying
the validity of logic which, they think, has been superseded by dialectic.
This way I have tried to block in 'What is Dialectic?', *Mind*, vol. 49 N.S.,
pp. 403 ff.

[2] See K. Mannheim, *op. cit.*, p. 202. It may be mentioned that a
psychological holism is at present very fashionable with educational
theorists.

[3] The doctrine that history deals with 'concrete individual wholes',
which may be persons or events or epochs, was propagated especially
by Troeltsch. Its truth is constantly assumed by Mannheim.

it is interested. It is a mistake to believe that there can
be a history in the holistic sense, a history of 'States of
Society' which represent 'the whole of the social organism' or 'all the social and historical events of an
epoch'. This idea derives from an intuitive view of a
history of mankind as a vast and comprehensive stream
of development. But such a history cannot be written.
Every written history is a history of a certain narrow
aspect of this 'total' development, and is anyhow a very
incomplete history even of the particular incomplete
aspect chosen.

The holistic tendencies of Utopianism and of historicism are unified in the following characteristic
statement: 'We have never had to set up and direct
the entire system of nature as completely as we are
forced to do to-day with our society, and *therefore* we
have never had to penetrate into the history and structure of the individual worlds of nature. Mankind is
tending . . . to regulate the whole of its social life
although it has never attempted to undertake the
creation of a second nature . . .'[1] This statement
illustrates the mistaken belief that if we wish, as holists,
to treat 'the entire system of nature completely', it
will be helpful to adopt a historical method. But the
natural sciences, such as geology, which have adopted
this method are far from grasping the 'entire system'
of their subject-matter. Also illustrated by this statement is the incorrect view that it is possible to 'set up'
or 'direct' or 'regulate' or 'create' wholes in sense (*a*).
That 'we have never had to set up and direct the entire system of nature' is certainly true, simply because
we cannot even set up and direct one single piece of
physical apparatus in its 'entirety'. Such things cannot
be done. They are Utopian dreams, or perhaps misunderstandings. And to tell us that we are *forced* to-day

[1] K. Mannheim, *op. cit.*, p. 175 f. (italics mine).

to do a thing which is logically impossible, namely to set up and direct the entire system of society, and to regulate the whole of social life, is merely a typical attempt to threaten us with 'historical forces' and 'impending developments' which make Utopian planning inevitable.

Incidentally, the statement quoted is interesting as an admission of the very significant fact that there exists no physical analogy of holistic engineering or of the corresponding 'science'. The pursuit of the analogy between natural and social science is therefore certainly helpful in clarifying the issue here.

Such is the logical status of holism, the rock on which we are encouraged to build a new world.

A critical remark may be added on wholes in sense (*b*), which I have admitted to scientific status. Without retracting anything I have said, I must point out that the triviality as well as the vagueness of the statement that the whole is more than the sum of its parts seems to be seldom realized. Even three apples on a plate are more than 'a mere sum', in so far as there must be certain relations between them (the biggest may or may not lie between the others, etc.): relations which do not follow from the fact that there are three apples, and which can be studied scientifically. Also, the much advertised opposition between the 'atomistic' and the '*Gestalt*' approach is entirely baseless, at least as far as atomic physics is concerned: for atomic physics does **not** merely 'sum up' its elementary particles, but studies particle *systems* from a point of view most definitely concerned with wholes in sense (*b*).[1]

---

[1] See, for example, Pauli's exclusion principle.—To the social scientist, such ideas as competition or division of labour should make it abundantly clear that an 'atomistic' or 'individualistic' approach in no way prevents us from recognizing that every individual interacts with all others. (In psychology the situation is different, because atomism seems to be inapplicable there—in spite of many attempts to apply it.)

What most of the *Gestalt* theorists apparently wish to assert is the existence of two kinds of things, 'heaps', in which we cannot discern any order, and 'wholes', in which an order or symmetry or a regularity or a system or a structural plan may be found. Thus, a sentence such as 'Organisms are wholes' reduces itself to the triviality that, in an organism, we can discern some order. Besides, a so-called 'heap', as a rule, has a *Gestalt* aspect too, just as much as the often cited example of the electrical field. (Consider the regular manner in which pressure increases within a heap of stones.) Thus the distinction is not only trivial, but exceedingly vague; and is not applicable to different kinds of things, but merely to different aspects of the same things.

24   THE HOLISTIC THEORY OF SOCIAL EXPERIMENTS

Holistic thinking is particularly detrimental in its influence upon the historicist theory of social experiments (expounded above in section 2). Although the piecemeal technologist will agree with the historicist view that large-scale or holistic social experiments, if at all possible, are extremely unsuitable for scientific purposes, he will emphatically deny the assumption, common to both historicism and Utopianism, that social experiments, in order to be realistic, must be of the character of Utopian attempts at re-modelling the whole of society.

It is convenient to begin our criticism with the discussion of a very obvious objection to the Utopian programme, namely that we do not possess the experimental knowledge needed for such an undertaking. The blueprints of the physical engineer are based on an

experimental technology; all the principles that underlie his activities are tested by practical experiments.
But the holistic blueprints of the social engineer are
not based on any comparable practical experience.
Thus the alleged analogy between physical engineering
and holistic social engineering breaks down; holistic
planning is rightly described as 'Utopian', since the
scientific basis of its plans is simply nowhere.

Faced with this criticism, the Utopian engineer is
likely to admit the need for practical experience, and
for an experimental technology. But he will claim that
we shall never know anything about these matters if
we shrink from making social experiments, or, what
in his view amounts to the same thing, from holistic
engineering. We must make a beginning, he will argue,
using whatever knowledge we possess, be it great or
small. If we have some knowledge of aircraft designing
to-day, it is only because some pioneer who did not
possess this knowledge dared to design an aircraft and
to try it out. Thus the Utopianist may even contend
that the holistic method which he advocates is nothing
but the experimental method applied to society. For
he holds, in common with the historicist, that small-
scale experiments, such as an experiment in socialism
carried out in a factory or in a village or even in a
district, would be quite inconclusive; such isolated
'Robinson-Crusoe experiments' cannot tell us anything about modern social life in the 'Great Society'.
They even deserve the nick-name 'Utopian'—in the
(Marxist) sense in which this term implies the neglect
of historical tendencies. (The implication in this case
would be that the tendency towards an increasing
interdependence of social life is being neglected.)

We see that Utopianism and historicism agree in the
view that *a social experiment (if there is such a thing) could
be of value only if carried out on a holistic scale.* This widely

84

held prejudice involves the belief that we are seldom in the position to carry out 'planned experiments' in the social field, and that, for an account of the results of 'chance experiments', so far carried out in this field, we have to turn to *history*.[1]

I have two objections against this view: (*a*) that it overlooks those *piecemeal experiments* which are fundamental for all social knowledge, pre-scientific as well as scientific; (*b*) that *holistic experiments* are unlikely to contribute much to our experimental knowledge; and that they can be called 'experiments' only in the sense in which this term is synonymous with *an action whose outcome is uncertain*, but not in the sense in which this term is used to denote *a means of acquiring knowledge, by comparing the results obtained with the results expected*.

Concerning (*a*) it may be pointed out that the holistic view of social experiments leaves unexplained the fact that we possess a very great deal of experimental knowledge of social life. There is a difference between an experienced and an inexperienced business man, or organizer, or politician, or general. It is a difference in their social experience; and in experience gained not merely through observation, or by reflecting upon what they have observed, but by efforts to achieve some practical aim. It must be admitted that the knowledge attained in this way is usually of a pre-scientific kind, and therefore more like knowledge gained by casual observation than knowledge gained by carefully designed scientific experiments; but this is no reason for denying that the knowledge in question is based on experiment rather than on mere

[1] This was also Mill's view when he said of social experiments that 'we palpably never have the power of trying any. We can only watch those which nature produces, . . . the successions of phenomena recorded in history . . .' (see *Logic*, Book VI, ch. VII, section 2).

observation. A grocer who opens a new shop is conducting a social experiment; and even a man who joins a queue before a theatre gains experimental technological knowledge which he may utilize by having his seat reserved next time, which again is a social experiment. And we should not forget that only practical experiments have taught buyers and sellers on the markets the lesson that prices are liable to be lowered by every increase of supply, and raised by every increase of demand.

Examples of piecemeal experiments on a somewhat larger scale would be the decision of a monopolist to change the price of his product; the introduction, whether by a private or a public insurance company, of a new type of health or employment insurance; or the introduction of a new sales tax, or of a policy to combat trade cycles. All these experiments are carried out with practical rather than scientific aims in view. Moreover, experiments have been carried out by some large firms with the deliberate aim of increasing their knowledge of the market (in order to increase profits at a later stage, of course) rather than with the aim of increasing their profits immediately.[1] The situation is very similar to that of physical engineering and to the pre-scientific methods by which our technological knowledge in matters such as the building of ships or the art of navigation was first acquired. There seems to be no reason why these methods should not be improved on, and ultimately replaced by a more

---

[1] Sidney and Beatrice Webb, *Methods of Social Study* (1932), pp. 221 ff., give similar examples of social experiments. They do not distinguish, however, between the two kinds of experiments which are here called 'piecemeal' and 'holistic', although their criticism of the experimental method (see p. 226, 'intermixture of effects') is especially cogent as a criticism of holistic experiments (which they seem to admire). Furthermore, their criticism is combined with the 'variability argument' which I consider to be invalid; see section 25, below.

scientifically minded technology; that is to say, by more systematic approach in the same direction, based on critical thought as well as on experiment.

According to this piecemeal view, there is no clearly marked division between the pre-scientific and the scientific experimental approaches, even though the more and more conscious application of scientific, that is to say, of critical methods, is of great importance. Both approaches may be described, fundamentally, as utilizing the method of trial and error. We try; that is, we do not merely register an observation, but make active attempts to solve some more or less practical and definite problems. And we make progress if, and only if, we are prepared to *learn from our mistakes*: to recognize our errors and to utilize them critically instead of persevering in them dogmatically. Though this analysis may sound trivial, it describes, I believe, the method of all empirical sciences. This method assumes a more and more scientific character the more freely and consciously we are prepared to risk a trial, and the more critically we watch for the mistakes we always make. And this formula covers not only the method of experiment, but also the relationship between theory and experiment. All theories are trials; they are tentative hypotheses, tried out to see whether they work; and all experimental corroboration is simply the result of tests undertaken in a critical spirit, in an attempt to find out where our theories err.[1]

For the piecemeal technologist or engineer these views mean that, if he wishes to introduce scientific methods into the study of society and into politics, what is needed most is the adoption of a critical

[1] A fuller analysis of the methods of modern physics on the lines here indicated may be found in my *Logic of Scientific Discovery*; see also 'What is Dialectic?', *Mind*, vol. 49, pp. 403 ff. See also, for example, Tinbergen, *Statistical Testing of Business Cycle Theories*, vol. II, p. 21: 'The construction of a model . . . is . . . a matter of trial and error', etc.

attitude, and the realization that not only trial but also error is necessary. And he must learn not only to expect mistakes, but consciously to search for them. We all have an unscientific weakness for being always in the right, and this weakness seems to be particularly common among professional and amateur politicians. But the only way to apply something like scientific method in politics is to proceed on the assumption that there can be no political move which has no drawbacks, no undesirable consequences. To look out for these mistakes, to find them, to bring them into the open, to analyse them, and to learn from them, this is what a scientific politician as well as a political scientist must do. Scientific method in politics means that the great art of convincing ourselves that we have not made any mistakes, of ignoring them, of hiding them, and of blaming others for them, is replaced by the greater art of accepting the responsibility for them, of trying to learn from them, and of applying this knowledge so that we may avoid them in the future.

We now turn to point (*b*), the criticism of the view that we can learn from holistic experiments, or more precisely, from measures carried out on a scale that approaches the holistic dream (for holistic experiments in the radical sense that they re-model 'the whole of society' are logically impossible, as I showed in the foregoing section). Our main point is very simple: it is difficult enough to be critical of our own mistakes, but it must be nearly impossible for us to persist in a critical attitude towards those of our actions which involve the lives of many men. To put it differently, it is very hard to learn from very big mistakes.

The reasons for this are twofold; they are technical as well as moral. Since so much is done at a time, it is impossible to say which particular measure is responsible for any of the results; or rather, if we do attribute a certain result to a certain measure, then we can do so only on the basis of some theoretical knowledge gained previously, and not from the holistic experiment in question. This experiment does not help us to attribute particular results to particular measures; all we can do is to attribute the 'whole result' to it; and whatever this may mean, it is certainly difficult to assess. Even the greatest efforts to secure a well-informed, independent, and critical statement of these results are unlikely to prove successful. But the chances that such efforts will be made are negligible; on the contrary, there is every likelihood that free discussion about the holistic plan and its consequences will not be tolerated. The reason is that every attempt at planning on a very large scale is an undertaking which must cause considerable inconvenience to many people, to put it mildly, and over a considerable span of time. Accordingly there will always be a tendency to oppose the plan, and to complain about it. To many of these complaints the Utopian engineer will have to turn a deaf ear if he wishes to get anywhere at all; in fact, it will be part of his business to suppress unreasonable objections. But with them he must invariably suppress reasonable criticism too. And the mere fact that expressions of dissatisfaction will have to be curbed reduces even the most enthusiastic expression of satisfaction to insignificance. Thus it will be difficult to ascertain the facts, i.e. the repercussions of the plan on the individual citizen; and without these facts scientific criticism is impossible.

But the difficulty of combining holistic planning with scientific methods is still more fundamental than has so far been indicated. The holistic planner overlooks the fact that it is easy to centralize power but impossible to centralize all that knowledge which is distributed over many individual minds, and whose centralization would be necessary for the wise wielding of centralized power.[1] But this fact has far-reaching consequences. Unable to ascertain what is in the minds of so many individuals, he must try to simplify his problems by eliminating individual differences: he must try to control and stereotype interests and beliefs by education and propaganda.[2] But this attempt to exercise power over minds must destroy the last possibility of finding out what people really think, for it is clearly incompatible with the free expression of thought, especially of critical thought. Ultimately, it must destroy knowledge; and the greater the gain in power, the greater will be the loss of knowledge. (Political power and social knowledge may thus be discovered to be 'complementary' in Bohr's sense of the term. And it may even turn out to be the only clear illustration of this elusive but fashionable term.[3])

[1] The observation that it is impossible to have the knowledge needed for planning 'concentrated anywhere in a single head' is due to Hayek; see *Collectivist Economic Planning*, p. 210. (See also note 1 on p. 64, above.)

[2] One of the most crucial points in Spinoza's political theory is the impossibility of knowing and of controlling what other people think. He defines 'tyranny' as the attempt to achieve the impossible, and to exercise power where it cannot be exercised. Spinoza, it must be remembered, was not exactly a liberal; he did not believe in institutional control of power, but thought that a prince has a right to exercise his powers up to their actual limit. Yet what Spinoza calls 'tyranny', and declares to be in conflict with reason, is treated quite innocently by holistic planners as a 'scientific' problem, the 'problem of transforming men'.

[3] Niels Bohr calls two approaches 'complementary' if they are (*a*) complementary in the usual sense and (*b*) if they are exclusive of each other in the sense that the more we make use of the one the less we can use the other. Although I refer in the text mainly to *social* knowledge, it may be claimed that the accumulation (and concentration) of political power is 'complementary' to the progress of scientific knowledge in general. For the progress of science depends on free competition of thought, hence on freedom of thought, and hence, ultimately, on political freedom.

All these remarks are confined to the problem of scientific method. They tacitly grant the colossal assumption that we need not question the fundamental benevolence of the planning Utopian engineer, who is vested with an authority which at least approaches dictatorial powers. Tawney concludes a discussion of Luther and his time with the words: 'Sceptical as to the existence of unicorns and salamanders, the age of Machiavelli and Henry VIII found food for its credulity in the worship of that rare monster, the God-fearing Prince.'[1] Replace here the words 'unicorns and salamanders' by 'the God-fearing Prince'; replace the two names by those of some of their more obvious modern counterparts, and the phrase 'the God-fearing Prince' by 'the benevolent planning authority': and you have a description of the credulity of our own time. This credulity will not be challenged here; yet it may be remarked that, assuming the unlimited and unvarying benevolence of the powerful planners, our analysis shows that it may be impossible for them ever to find out whether the results of their measures tally with their good intentions.

I do not believe that any corresponding criticism of the piecemeal method can be offered. This method can be used, more particularly, in order to search for, and fight against, the greatest and most urgent evils of society, rather than to seek, and to fight for, some ultimate good (as holists are inclined to do). But a systematic fight against definite wrongs, against concrete forms of injustice or exploitation, and avoidable suffering such as poverty or unemployment, is a very different thing from the attempt to realize a distant ideal blueprint of society. Success or failure is more easily appraised, and there is no inherent reason why

[1] R. H. Tawney, *Religion and The Rise of Capitalism*, ch. II, end of section ii.

this method should lead to an accumulation of power, and to the suppression of criticism. Also, such a fight against concrete wrongs and concrete dangers is more likely to find the support of a great majority than a fight for the establishment of a Utopia, ideal as it may appear to the planners. This may perhaps throw some light on the fact that in democratic countries defending themselves against aggression, sufficient support may be forthcoming for the necessary far-reaching measures (which may even take on the character of holistic planning) *without suppression of public criticism*, while in countries preparing for an attack or waging an aggressive war, public criticism as a rule must be suppressed, in order that public support may be mobilized by presenting aggression as defence.

We may now turn back to the Utopianist's claim that his method is the true experimental method applied to the field of sociology. This claim, I think, is dispelled by our criticism. This can be further illustrated by the analogy between physical and holistic engineering. It may be admitted that physical machines can be successfully planned by way of blueprints, and with them, even a whole plant for their production, etc. But all this is possible only because many piecemeal experiments have been carried out beforehand. Every machine is the result of a great many small improvements. Every model must be 'developed' by the method of trial and error, by countless small adjustments. The same holds for the planning of the production plant. The apparently holistic plan can succeed only because we have made all kinds of small mistakes already; otherwise there is every reason to expect that it would lead to big mistakes.

Thus the analogy between physical and social engineering, if looked into more closely, turns against the holist and in favour of the piecemeal social engineer.

The expression 'social engineering', which alludes to this analogy, has been usurped by the Utopianist without a shadow of right.

With this, I conclude my critical remarks on Utopianism, and shall now concentrate my attack on its ally, historicism. I believe I have now given a sufficient answer to the historicist's contention concerning social experiments, except for the argument that social experiments are useless because it is impossible to repeat them under precisely similar conditions. We will now consider this argument.

25   THE VARIABILITY OF EXPERIMENTAL CONDITIONS

The historicist contends that the experimental method cannot be applied to the social sciences because we cannot, in the social field, reproduce at will precisely similar experimental conditions. This brings us a little closer to the heart of the historicist position. I admit that there may be something in this contention: no doubt there are some differences here between physical and sociological methods. Nevertheless, I assert that the historicist contention rests upon a gross misunderstanding of the experimental methods of physics.

Let us first consider these methods. Every experimental physicist knows that very dissimilar things may happen under what appear to be precisely similar conditions. Two wires may at first sight look exactly alike, but if the one is exchanged for the other in a piece of electrical apparatus, the resulting difference may be very great. Upon closer inspection (say, through a microscope), we may perhaps find that they were not as similar as they first appeared. But often it is very hard indeed to detect a difference in the conditions of the two experiments that lead to different

results. Long research, experimental as well as theoretical, may be needed in order to find what kind of
similarity is relevant, and what degree of similarity
sufficient. This research may have to be carried out
before we are able to secure similar conditions for
our experiments, and before we even know what
'similar conditions' means in this case. And yet, *the
method of experiment is applied all the time.*

Thus we can say that the question of what are to be
described as 'similar conditions' depends on the kind
of experiment, and can be answered only by using
experiments. It is impossible to decide *a priori* about
any observed difference or similarity, however striking,
whether or not it will be relevant for the purpose of
reproducing an experiment. So we must allow the
experimental method to take care of itself. Precisely
analogous considerations hold for the much debated
problem of the artificial *isolation* of experiments from
disturbing influences. Clearly, we cannot isolate a
piece of apparatus against *all* influences; for example,
we cannot know *a priori* whether the influence of the
position of the planets or of the moon upon a physical
experiment is considerable or negligible. What kind
of artificial isolation, if any, is needed, we can learn
only from the result of experiments, or from theories
which, in turn, are tested by experiments.

In the light of such considerations, the historicist
argument that social experiments are fatally hampered
by the variability of social conditions, and especially
by the changes which are due to historical developments, loses its force. The striking differences with
which the historicist is so much preoccupied, that is to
say, the differences between the conditions prevalent
in various historical periods, need not create any difficulties peculiar to social science. It may be admitted
that if we were suddenly transported into another

historical period, we should probably find that many of our social expectations, formed on the basis of piecemeal experiments made in our society, are disappointed. In other words, experiments may lead to unforeseen results. But it would be *experiments* which led us to discover the change in social conditions; experiments would teach us that certain social conditions vary with the *historical period*; just as experiments have taught the physicist that the temperature of boiling water may vary with *the geographical position*.[1] In other words, the doctrine of the difference between historical periods, far from making social experiments impossible, is merely an expression of the assumption that, if shifted into another period, we should continue to make our piecemeal experiments, but with surprising or disappointing results. In fact, if we know anything about different attitudes in different historical periods, then it is from experiments, carried out in our imagination. Historians find difficulties in interpreting certain records, or they discover facts showing that some of their predecessors had misinterpreted some historical evidence. These difficulties of historical interpretation are our only evidence of the kind of historical change the historicist has in mind; yet they are nothing but discrepancies between the expected and the actual results of our thought experiments. It is these surprises and disappointments which, by the method of trial and error, have led to improvements in our ability to interpret strange social conditions. And what in the case of historical interpretation we achieve by thought-experiment has been achieved by anthropologists in

[1] In both cases—historical periods and geographical positions—we may find, using theories tested by experiments, that any reference to temporal or spatial locations can be replaced by some *general* description of certain prevailing relevant conditions, such as the state of education, or the altitude.

practical field work. Those modern investigators who have succeeded in adjusting their expectations to conditions which are perhaps no less remote than those of the Stone Age, owe their success to piecemeal experiments.

Some historicists doubt the possibility of such successful adjustments; and they even defend their doctrine of the futility of social experiments by the argument that, if shifted to remote historical periods, far too many of our social experiments would lead to disappointment. They assert that we should be unable to adjust our habits of thought, and especially our habits of analysing social events, to these bewildering conditions. Such fears seem to me part of the historicist hysteria—the obsession with the importance of social change; but I must admit that it would be difficult to dispel those fears on *a priori* grounds. After all, the ability to adjust oneself to a new environment varies from person to person, and there seems to be no reason why we should expect of a historicist (who holds such defeatist views) that he will be able to adapt his mind successfully to changes in the social environment. Also, matters will depend on the character of the new environment. The possibility that a social investigator may find himself being eaten before he succeeds in adjusting himself, by trial and error, to cannibal habits, cannot be excluded any more than the possibility that, in some 'planned' society, his investigations may end in a concentration camp. Yet analogous remarks hold for the realm of physics. There are many places in the world where physical conditions prevail which offer to the physicist little chance of survival, or of adjusting himself to these conditions by trial and error.

To sum up, there does not seem any basis for the plausible historicist assertion that the variability of historical conditions renders the experimental method inapplicable to the problems of society, or for the assertion that, in this point, the study of society is fundamentally different from the study of nature. It is quite another matter if we admit that, in practice, it is often very difficult for the social scientist to choose and to vary his experimental conditions at will. The physicist is in a better position although he too is sometimes faced by similar difficulties. Thus the possibilities of carrying out experiments in varying gravitational fields, or under extreme temperature conditions, are very limited. But we must not forget that many possibilities which are open to the physicist today were impracticable not long ago, not because of physical but because of social difficulties, i.e. because we were not prepared to risk the money needed for research. It is a fact, however, that very many physical investigations can now be carried out under experimental conditions which leave little to be desired, while the social scientist is in a very different position. Many experiments which would be most desirable will remain dreams for a long time to come, in spite of the fact that they are not of a Utopian but of a piecemeal character. In practice, he must rely too often on experiments carried out mentally, and on an analysis of political measures carried out under conditions, and in a manner, which leave much to be desired from the scientific point of view.

26 ARE GENERALIZATIONS CONFINED TO PERIODS?

The fact that I have discussed the problem of social experiments before discussing at any length the problem of sociological laws, or theories, or hypotheses, or 'generalizations', does not mean that I think that observations and experiments are in some way or other logically prior to theories. On the contrary, I believe that theories are prior to observations as well as to experiments, in the sense that the latter are significant only in relation to theoretical problems. Also, we must have a question before we can hope that observation or experiment may help us in any way to provide an answer. Or to put it in terms of the method of trial and error, the trial must come before the error; and as we have seen (in section 24), the theory or hypothesis, which is always tentative, is part of the trial, while observation and experiment help us to weed out theories by showing where they err. I do not believe, therefore, in the 'method of generalization', that is to say, in the view that science begins with observations from which it derives its theories by some process of generalization or induction. I believe, rather, that the function of observation and experiment is the more modest one of helping us to test our theories and to eliminate those which do not stand up to tests; even though it must be admitted that this process of weeding out not only checks theoretical speculation, but also stimulates it to try again—and often to err again, and to be refuted again, by new observations and experiments.

In this section, I shall criticize the historicist contention (see section 1) that in the social sciences the validity of all generalizations, or at least of the most important ones, is confined to the concrete historical period in which the relevant observations were made. I shall criticize this contention without first discussing the question whether or not the so-called 'method of generalization' is defensible, in spite of my conviction that it is not; for I think that the historicist contention can be refuted without showing that this method is invalid. The discussion of my views on this method, and on the relations between theory and experiment in general, can therefore be postponed. It will be taken up again in section 28.

I begin my criticism of the historicist contention with the admission that most people living in a certain historical period will incline to the erroneous belief that the regularities which they observe around them are universal laws of social life, holding good for all societies. Indeed, we sometimes only notice that we are cherishing such beliefs when, in a foreign country, we find that our habits regarding food, our greeting-taboos, etc., are by no means as acceptable as we naïvely assumed. It is a rather obvious inference that many of our other generalizations, whether consciously held or not, may be of the same kind, though they may remain unchallenged because we cannot travel into another historical period. (This inference was drawn, for example, by Hesiod.[1]) In other words, it must be admitted that there may be many regularities in our social life which are characteristic of our particular period only, and that we are inclined to overlook this limitation. So that (especially in a time of rapid social change) we may learn to our sorrow that we have relied on laws that have lost their validity.[2]

If the historicist's contentions went no further than this, we could only accuse him of labouring a rather

---

[1] The same inference is also the basis of the so-called '*sociology of knowledge*', criticized here on pp. 155 f., and in ch. 23 of my *Open Society*.

[2] K. Mannheim, *Man and Society*, p. 178, writes of 'the layman who observes the social world intelligently', that 'in static periods he is unable, in any case, to distinguish between a general abstract social law and particular principles which obtain only in a certain epoch, since in periods of only slight variability, the divergences between these two types do not become clear to the observer.' Mannheim calls these particular principles which obtain only in a certain epoch '*principia media*'; see note 2 on p. 101, below. For the situation 'in an age where the social structure is changing through and through', see Mannheim, *op. cit.*, p. 179 f.

trivial point. But unfortunately, he asserts more. He insists that the situation creates difficulties which do not occur in the natural sciences; and more particularly that, in contrast to the natural sciences, in the social sciences we must never assume that we have discovered a truly universal law, since we can never know whether it always held good in the past (for our records may be insufficient), or whether it will always hold good in the future.

In opposition to such claims, I do not admit that the situation described is in any way peculiar to the social sciences, or that it creates any particular difficulties. On the contrary, it is obvious that a change in our physical environment may give rise to experiences which are quite analogous to those which arise from a change in our social or historical environment. Can there be a more obvious and proverbial regularity than the succession of day and night? Yet, it breaks down if we cross the polar circle. It is perhaps a little difficult to compare physical with social experiences, but I think that such a breakdown may be quite as startling as any that might occur in the social realm. To take another example, the historical or social environments of Crete in 1900 and of Crete three thousand years ago can hardly be said to differ more than the geographical or physical environments of Crete and of Greenland. A sudden unprepared removal from one physical environment into the other would, I think, be more likely to produce fatal results than a corresponding change in the social environment.

It seems clear to me that the historicist overrates the significance of the somewhat spectacular differences between various historical periods, and that he underrates the possibilities of scientific ingenuity. It is true that the laws discovered by Kepler are valid only for planetary systems, but their validity is not confined to the Solar system in which Kepler lived, and which he observed.[1] Newton did not have to withdraw into a part of the universe where he could observe moving bodies that were free from the influence of gravitational and other forces in order to see the importance of the law of inertia. On the other hand, this law, even though no body in this system moves in accordance with it, does not lose its significance within the Solar system. Similarly, there seems no reason why we should be unable to frame sociological theories which are important for all social periods. The spectacular differences between these periods are no indication that such laws cannot be found, any more than the spectacular differences between Greenland and Crete can prove that there are no physical laws which hold for both regions. On the contrary, these differences seem to be, in some cases at least, of a comparatively superficial character (such as are differences in habits, in greeting, ritual, etc.), and more or less the same seems to hold good of those regularities which are said to be characteristic of a certain historical period or of a certain society (and which are now called *principia media* by some sociologists).[2]

[1] Kepler's laws are chosen by Mill as examples of what he calls, following Bacon, '*axiomata media*', for the reason that they are not general laws of motion but only (approximate) laws of planetary motion: see *Logic*, Book VI, ch. V, section 5. Analogous *axiomata media* of a social science would be laws which hold for all 'social systems' *of a certain kind*, rather than the more accidental regularities of a historically given period. The latter might be compared, not with Kepler's laws, but, for example, with regularities in the order of the planets of our particular solar system.

[2] K. Mannheim, *op. cit.*, p. 177, introduces the expression '*principia media*' with reference to Mill (who speaks of *axiomata media*; see the preceding note) in order to denote what I have called 'generalizations confined to the concrete historical period in which the relevant observations were made'; see, for example, his passage (*op. cit.*, p. 178; cp. my note 2 on p. 99 above): 'The layman who observes the social world intelligently

To this, the historicist may reply that the differences in social environment are more fundamental than the differences in physical environment; for if society changes, man changes too; and this implies a change in all regularities, since all social regularities depend on the nature of man, the atom of society. Our answer is that physical atoms also change with their environment (for example, under the influence of electro-magnetic fields, etc.), not in defiance of the laws of physics, but in accordance with these laws. Besides, the significance of the alleged changes of human nature is dubious, and very hard to assess.

We now turn to the historicist contention that in the social sciences we must never assume that we have discovered a truly universal law since we cannot be sure whether its validity extends beyond the periods in which we have observed it to hold. This may be admitted, but only in so far as it applies to the natural sciences as well. In the natural sciences, it is clear, we can never be quite certain whether our laws are really universally valid, or whether they hold only in a certain period (perhaps only in the period during which the universe expands) or only in a certain region

understands events primarily by the unconscious use of such *principia media*', which are ' . . . particular principles which obtain only in a certain epoch'. (Mannheim, *loc. cit.*, defines his *principia media* by saying that they are 'in the last analysis universal forces in a concrete setting as they become integrated out of the various factors at work in a given place at a given time—a particular combination of circumstances which may never be repeated'.) Mannheim states that he does not follow 'historicism, Hegelianism, and Marxism' in their failure to take 'universal factors into account' (*op. cit.*, p. 177 f.). Accordingly, his position is one of insisting on the importance of generalizations confined to concrete or individual historical periods, while admitting that we may proceed from them, by a 'method of abstraction', to 'the general principles which are contained in them'. (In opposition to this view, I do not believe that the more general theories can be obtained by abstraction from those regularities of habits, legal procedures, etc., which, according to the examples given by Mannheim on pp. 179 ff., constitute his *principia media*.)

(perhaps in a region of comparatively weak gravitational fields). In spite of the impossibility of making sure of their universal validity, we do not add in our formulation of natural laws a condition saying that they are asserted only for the period for which they have been observed to hold, or perhaps only within 'the present cosmological period'. It would not be a sign of laudable scientific caution if we were to add such a condition, but a sign that we do not understand scientific procedure.[1] For it is an important postulate of scientific method that we should search for laws with an unlimited realm of validity.[2] If we were to admit laws that are themselves subject to change, change could never be explained by laws. It would be the admission that change is simply miraculous. And it would be the end of scientific progress; for if unexpected observations were made, there would be no need to revise our theories: the *ad hoc* hypothesis that the laws have changed would 'explain' everything.

These arguments hold for the social sciences no less than for the natural sciences.

[1] It has often been suggested that instead of vainly attempting to follow in sociology the example of physics, and to search for universal sociological laws, it would be better to follow in physics the example of a historicist sociology, i.e. to operate with laws which are limited to historical periods. Historicists who are anxious to emphasize the unity of physics and sociology are especially inclined to think on such lines. See Neurath, *Erkenntnis*, vol. VI, p. 399.

[2] It is the same postulate which in physics leads, for example, to the demand that the red shifts observed in distant nebulae should be *explained*; for without this postulate, it would be quite sufficient to assume that the laws of atomic frequencies change with the different regions of the universe, or with time. And it is the same postulate which leads the theory of relativity to express the laws of motion, such as the law of addition of velocities, etc., uniformly for high and low velocities (or for strong and weak gravitational fields) and to be dissatisfied with *ad hoc* assumptions for different realms of velocity (or of gravitation). For a discussion of this postulate of the 'Invariance of Natural Laws', and its opposition to that of the 'Uniformity of Nature', see my *Logic of Scientific Discovery*, section 79.

With this I conclude my criticism of the more fundamental among the anti-naturalistic doctrines of historicism. Before proceeding to discuss some of the less fundamental ones, I shall turn next to one of the pro-naturalistic doctrines, namely, that we should search for the laws of historical development.

IV

CRITICISM OF
THE PRO-NATURALISTIC
DOCTRINES

27   IS THERE A LAW OF EVOLUTION?
LAWS AND TRENDS

THE doctrines of historicism which I have called
'*pro-naturalistic*' have much in common with its
anti-naturalistic doctrines. They are, for example,
influenced by holistic thinking, and they spring from
a misunderstanding of the methods of the natural
sciences. Since they represent a misguided effort to
copy these methods, they may be described as 'scientistic' (in Professor Hayek's sense [1]). They are just as
characteristic of historicism as are its anti-naturalistic
doctrines, and perhaps even more important. The
belief, more especially, that it is the task of the social

---

[1] See F. A. von Hayek, 'Scientism and the Study of Society', *Economica*,
N.S., vol. IX, especially p. 269. Professor Hayek uses the term 'scientism'
as a name for 'the slavish imitation of the method and language of
science'. Here it is used, rather, as a name for the imitation of *what
certain people mistake* for the method and language of science.

sciences to lay bare the *law of evolution of society* in order to foretell its future (a view expounded in sections 14 to 17, above) might be perhaps described as the central historicist doctrine. For it is this view of a society moving through a series of periods that gives rise, on the one hand, to the contrast between a changing social and an unchanging physical world, and thereby to anti-naturalism. On the other hand, it is the same view that gives rise to the pro-naturalistic—and scientistic—belief in so-called 'natural laws of succession'; a belief which, in the days of Comte and Mill, could claim to be supported by the long-term predictions of astronomy, and more recently, by Darwinism. Indeed, the recent vogue of historicism might be regarded as merely part of the vogue of evolutionism—a philosophy that owes its influence largely to the somewhat sensational clash between a brilliant scientific hypothesis concerning the history of the various species of animals and plants on earth, and an older metaphysical theory which, incidentally, happened to be part of an established religious belief.[1]

What we call the evolutionary hypothesis is an explanation of a host of biological and paleontological observations—for instance, of certain similarities between various species and genera—by the assumption of the common ancestry of related forms.[2] This hypo-

[1] I agree with Professor Raven when, in his *Science, Religion, and the Future* (1943), he calls this conflict 'a storm in a Victorian tea-cup'; though the force of this remark is perhaps a little impaired by the attention he pays to the vapours still emerging from the cup—to the Great Systems of Evolutionist Philosophy, produced by Bergson, Whitehead, Smuts, and others.

[2] Feeling somewhat intimidated by the tendency of evolutionists to suspect anyone of obscurantism who does not share their emotional attitude towards evolution as a 'daring and revolutionary challenge to traditional thought', I had better say here that I see in modern Darwinism the most successful explanation of the relevant facts. A good illustration of the emotional attitude of evolutionists is C. H. Waddington's statement

thesis is not a universal law, even though certain universal laws of nature, such as laws of heredity, segregation, and mutation, enter with it into the explanation. It has, rather, the character of a particular (singular or specific) historical statement. (It is of the same status as the historical statement: 'Charles Darwin and Francis Galton had a common grandfather'.) The fact that the evolutionary hypothesis is not a universal law of nature [1] but a particular (or, more precisely, singular) historical statement about the ancestry of a number of terrestrial plants and animals is somewhat obscured by the fact that the term 'hypothesis' is so often used to characterize the status of universal laws of nature. But we should not forget that we quite frequently use this term in a different sense. For example, it would undoubtedly be correct to describe a tentative medical diagnosis as a hypothesis, even though such a hypothesis is of a singular and historical character rather than of the character of a universal law. In other words, the fact that all laws of nature are hypotheses must not distract our attention from the fact that not all hypotheses are laws, and that more especially historical hypotheses are, as a rule, not universal but singular statements about one individual event, or a number of such events.

But can there be a *law* of evolution? Can there be a

(*Science and Ethics*, 1942, p. 17) that 'we must accept the direction of evolution as good simply because it *is* good'; a statement which also illustrates the fact that the following revealing comment by Professor Bernal upon the Darwinian controversy (*ibid.*, p. 115) is still apposite: 'It was not . . . that science had to fight an external enemy, the Church; it was that the Church . . . was within the scientists themselves.'

[1] Even a statement such as 'All vertebrates have one common pair of ancestors' is not, in spite of the word 'all', a universal law of nature; for it refers to the vertebrates existing on earth, rather than to all organisms at any place and time which have that constitution which we consider as characteristic of vertebrates. See my *Logic of Scientific Discovery*, section 14 f.

scientific law in the sense intended by T. H. Huxley when he wrote: '. . . he must be a half-hearted philosopher who . . . doubts that science will sooner or later . . . become possessed of the law of evolution of organic forms—of the unvarying order of that great chain of causes and effects of which all organic forms, ancient and modern, are the links . . .'?[1]

I believe that the answer to this question must be 'No', and that the search for the law of the 'unvarying order' in evolution cannot possibly fall within the scope of scientific method, whether in biology or in sociology. My reasons are very simple. The evolution of life on earth, or of human society, is a unique historical process. Such a process, we may assume, proceeds in accordance with all kinds of causal laws, for example, the laws of mechanics, of chemistry, of heredity and segregation, of natural selection, etc. Its description, however, is not a law, but only a singular historical statement. Universal laws make assertions concerning some unvarying order, as Huxley puts it, i.e. concerning all processes of a certain kind; and although there is no reason why the observation of one single instance should not incite us to formulate a

---

[1] See T. H. Huxley, *Lay Sermons* (1880), p. 214. Huxley's belief in a law of evolution is very remarkable in view of his exceedingly critical attitude towards the idea of a law of (inevitable) progress. The explanation appears to be that he not only distinguished sharply between natural evolution and progress, but that he held (rightly, I believe) that these two had little to do with each other. Julian Huxley's interesting analysis of what he calls 'evolutionary progress' (*Evolution*, 1942, 559 ff.) seems to me to add little to this, although it is apparently designed to establish a link between evolution and progress. For he admits that evolution, though sometimes 'progressive', is more often not so. (For this, and for Huxley's definition of 'progress', see note 1 on p. 127, below.) The fact, on the other hand, that every 'progressive' development may be considered as evolutionary, is hardly more than trivial. (That the succession of dominant types is progressive in his sense may merely mean that we habitually apply the term 'dominant types' to those of the most successful types which are the most 'progressive'.)

universal law, nor why, if we are lucky, we should not
even hit upon the truth, it is clear that any law, formulated in this or in any other way, must be *tested* by new
instances before it can be taken seriously by science.
But we cannot hope to test a universal hypothesis nor
to find a natural law acceptable to science if we are for
ever confined to the observation of one unique process.
Nor can the observation of one unique process help us
to foresee its future development. The most careful
observation of *one* developing caterpillar will not help
us to predict its transformation into a butterfly. As
applied to the history of human society—and it is
with this that we are mainly concerned here—our
argument has been formulated by H. A. L. Fisher in
these words: 'Men . . . have discerned in history a plot,
a rhythm, a predetermined pattern . . . I can see only
one emergency following upon another . . . , *only one
great fact with respect to which, since it is unique, there can
be no generalizations . . .*' [1]

How can this objection be countered? There are,
in the main, two positions which may be taken up by
those who believe in a law of evolution. They may (*a*)
deny our contention that the evolutionary process is
unique; or (*b*) assert that in an evolutionary process,
even if it is unique, we may discern a trend or tendency
or direction, and that we may formulate a hypothesis
which states this trend, and test this hypothesis by
future experience. The two positions (*a*) and (*b*) are
not exclusive of each other.

Position (*a*) goes back to an idea of great antiquity
—the idea that the life-cycle of birth, childhood,
youth, maturity, old age, and death applies not only

[1] See H. A. L. Fisher's *History of Europe*, vol. I, p. vii (italics mine).
See also F. A. von Hayek, *op. cit.*, *Economica*, vol. X, p. 58, who criticizes
the attempt 'to find laws where in the nature of the case they cannot be
found, in the succession of the unique and singular historical phenomena'.

to individual animals and plants, but also to societies, races, and perhaps even to 'the whole world'. This ancient doctrine was used by Plato in his interpretation of the decline and fall of the Greek city states and of the Persian Empire.[1] Similar use of it has been made by Machiavelli, Vico, Spengler, and recently by Professor Toynbee in his imposing *Study of History*. From the point of view of this doctrine, history is repetitive, and the laws of the life-cycle of civilizations, for instance, can be studied in the same way as we study the life-cycle of a certain animal species.[2] It is a consequence of this doctrine, although one which its originators hardly intended, that our objection, based on the uniqueness of the evolutionary or historical process, loses its force. Now I do not intend to deny (nor, I feel certain, did Professor Fisher in the passage quoted) that history may sometimes repeat itself in certain respects, nor that the parallel between certain types of historical events, such as the rise of tyrannies in ancient Greece and in modern times, can be significant for the student of the sociology of political power.[3] But it is clear that all these instances of

[1] Plato describes the cycle of the Great Year in *The Statesman*; proceeding from the assumption that we live in the season of degeneration, he applies this doctrine in *The Republic* to the evolution of Greek cities, and in the *Laws* to the Persian Empire.

[2] Professor Toynbee insists that his method is to investigate *empirically* the life cycle of 21 odd specimens of the biological species 'civilization'. But even he does not seem to be influenced, in his adoption of this method, by any desire to counter Fisher's argument (quoted above); at least, I do not find any indication of such a desire in his comments on this argument which he is content to dismiss as an expression of 'the modern Western belief in the omnipotence of chance'; see *A Study of History*, vol. V, p. 414. I do not think that this characterization does justice to Fisher, who says in the continuation of the passage quoted: ' . . . The fact of progress is written plain and large on the page of history; but progress is not a law of nature. The ground gained by one generation may be lost by the next.'

[3] In biology, the position is similar in so far as a multiplicity of evolutions (e.g. of different genera) may be taken as the basis of *generaliza-*

repetition involve circumstances which are vastly dissimilar, and which may exert an important influence
upon further developments. We have therefore no
valid reason to expect of any apparent repetition of
a historical development that it will *continue* to run
parallel to its prototype. Admittedly, once we believe
in a law of repetitive life-cycles—a belief arrived at
by analogical speculations, or perhaps inherited from
Plato—we are sure to discover historical confirmation
of it nearly everywhere. But this is merely one of the
many instances of metaphysical theories seemingly
confirmed by facts—facts which, if examined more
closely, turn out to be selected in the light of the very
theories they are supposed to test.[1]

tions. But this comparison of evolutions has merely led to the description
of *types* of evolutionary processes. The position is the same as in social
history. We may find that certain types of events are repeated here or
there, but no law describing either the course of all evolutionary processes
(such as a law of evolutionary cycles) or the course of evolution in general
appears to result from such a comparison. See note 1 on p. 127, below.

[1] Of nearly every theory it may be said that it agrees with many facts:
this is one of the reasons why a theory can be said to be corroborated
only if we are unable to find refuting facts, rather than if we are able to
find supporting facts; see section 29, below, and my *Logic of Scientific
Discovery*, especially ch. X. An example of the procedure criticized
here is, I believe, Professor Toynbee's allegedly empirical investigation
into the life cycle of what he calls the 'species civilization' (see 2 on p. 110,
above). He seems to overlook the fact that he classifies as civilizations
only such entities as conform to his *a priori* belief in life cycles. For
example, Professor Toynbee contrasts (*op. cit.*, vol. I, pp. 147 to 149)
his 'civilizations' with 'primitive societies' in order to establish his
doctrine that these two cannot belong to the same 'species' although
they may belong to the same 'genus'. But the only basis of this classification is an *a priori* intuition into the nature of civilizations. This may be
seen from his argument that the two are obviously as different as are
elephants from rabbits—an intuitive argument whose weakness becomes
clear if we consider the case of a St. Bernard dog and a Pekingese. But the
whole question (whether or not the two belong to the same species) is
inadmissible, for it is based on the scientistic method of treating collec-
tives as if they were physical or biological bodies. Although this method
has often been criticized (see, for example, F. A. von Hayek, *Economica*,
vol. X, pp. 41 ff.) these criticisms have never received an adequate reply.

Turning to position (*b*), the belief that we may discern, and extrapolate, the trend or direction of an evolutionary movement, it may first be mentioned that this belief has influenced and has been used to support some of the cyclical hypotheses which represent position (*a*). Professor Toynbee, for example, expresses in support of position (*a*) the following views characteristic of (*b*): 'Civilizations are not static conditions of society but dynamic movements of an evolutionary kind. They not only cannot stand still, but they cannot reverse their direction without breaking down their own law of motion . . .'.[1] Here we have nearly all the elements usually found in statements of position (*b*): the idea of social *dynamics* (as opposed to social *statics*); of evolutionary *movements* of societies (under the influence of social *forces*); and of *directions* (and *courses*, and *velocities*) of such movements which, it is said, cannot be *reversed* without breaking the *laws of motion*. The terms in italics have all been taken over from physics into sociology, and their adoption has led to a series of misunderstandings which are of an astonishing crudity, but very characteristic of the scientistic misuse of the examples of physics and astronomy. Admittedly, these misunderstandings have done little harm outside the historicist workshop. In economics, for example, the use of the term '*dynamics*' (cp. the now fashionable term 'macro-dynamics') is unobjectionable, as must be admitted even by those who dislike the term. But even this use derives from Comte's attempt to apply to sociology the physicist's distinction between statics and dynamics; and there can be no doubt of the gross misunderstanding that underlies this attempt. *For the kind of society which the sociologist calls 'static' is precisely analogous to those physical systems which the physicist would call 'dynamic'* (although

[1] Toynbee, *op. cit.*, vol. I, p. 176.

'stationary'). A typical example is the solar system; it is the prototype of a dynamic system in the physicist's sense; but since it is repetitive (or 'stationary'), since it does not grow or develop, since it does not show any structural changes (apart from such changes as do not fall within the realm of celestial dynamics and which may therefore be neglected here), it corresponds, undoubtedly, to those social systems which the sociologist would call 'static'. The point is of considerable importance in connection with the claims of historicism, in so far as the success of the long-term predictions of astronomy depends entirely on this repetitive, and in the sociologist's sense static, character of the solar system—on the fact that we may here neglect any symptoms of a historical development. It is therefore certainly a mistake to suppose that these dynamical long-term predictions of a stationary system establish the possibility of large-scale historical prophecies of non-stationary social systems.

Very similar misunderstandings are involved in the application to society of the other terms from physics listed above. Often this application is quite harmless. No harm is done, for example, if we describe changes in social organization, in the methods of production, etc., as *movements*. But we ought to be clear that we are simply using a metaphor, and a rather misleading one at that. For if we speak in physics of the movement of a body or a system of bodies, then we do not intend to imply that the body or system in question undergoes any internal or structural change, but only that it changes its position relative to some (arbitrarily chosen) system of co-ordinates. As opposed to this, the sociologist means by a 'movement of society' some structural or internal change. He will, accordingly, assume that a movement of society is to be explained by *forces* while the physicist assumes that only *changes* of movement, but not movement as such, have to be so explained.[1] The ideas of the *speed* of a social movement, or of its *track*, or *course*, or *direction*, are similarly harmless as long as they are used merely in order to convey some intuitive impression; but if used with anything like scientific pretensions, they simply become scientistic jargon, or to be more precise, holistic jargon. Admittedly, any kind of change of a measurable social factor—for example, population growth—may be graphically represented as a track, just like the path of a moving body. But it is clear that such a diagram does not depict what people mean by the movement of society—considering that a stationary population may undergo a radical social upheaval. We may, of course, combine any number of such diagrams into one single multi-dimensional representation. But such a combined diagram cannot be said to represent the path of the movement of society; it does not tell us more than do the single ones together; it does not represent any movement of 'the whole society', but only changes of selected aspects. The idea of the movement of society itself—the idea that society, like a physical body, can move *as a whole* along a certain path and in a certain direction—is merely a holistic confusion.[2]

---

[1] This is so because of the law of inertia.—For an example of a typically 'scientistic' attempt to compute political 'forces' with the help of the Pythagorean theorem, see note 1 on p. 63, above.

[2] The confusion created by the talk about 'motion', 'force', 'direction', etc., may be gauged by considering that Henry Adams, the famous American historian, seriously hoped to determine the course of history by fixing the position of two points on its track—the one point located in the thirteenth century, the other in his own lifetime. He says himself of his project: 'With the help of these two points . . . he hoped to project his lines forward and backward indefinitely . . .', for, he argued, 'any schoolboy could see that man as a force must be measured by motion, from a fixed point' (*The Education of Henry Adams*, 1918, p. 434 f.). As a more recent example, I may quote Waddington's remark (*Science and*

The hope, more especially, that we may some day find the 'laws of motion of society', just as Newton found the laws of motion of physical bodies, is nothing but the result of these misunderstandings. Since there is no motion of society in any sense similar or analogous to the motion of physical bodies, there can be no such laws.

But, it will be said, the existence of trends or tendencies in social change can hardly be questioned: every statistician can calculate such trends. Are these trends not comparable with Newton's law of inertia? The answer is: trends exist, or more precisely, the assumption of trends is often a useful statistical device. *But trends are not laws.* A statement asserting the existence of a trend is existential, not universal. (A universal law, on the other hand, does not assert existence; on the contrary: as was shown at the end of section 20, it asserts the impossibility of something or other.[1]) And a statement asserting the existence of a trend at a certain time and place would be a singular historical statement, not a universal law. The practical significance of this logical situation is considerable: while we may base scientific predictions on laws, we cannot (as every cautious statistician knows) base them merely on the existence of trends. A trend (we may again take population growth as an example) which has persisted for hundreds or even thousands of years may change within a decade, or even more rapidly than that.

It is important to point out that *laws and trends are*

Ethics, p. 17 f.) that 'a social system' is 'something the existence of which essentially involves motion along an evolutionary path . . .', and that (p. 18 f.) 'the nature of science's contribution to ethics . . . is the revelation of the nature, the character and direction of the evolutionary process in the world as a whole . . .'

[1] See my *Logic of Scientific Discovery*, section 15, where reasons are given for considering existential statements to be *metaphysical* (in the sense of unscientific); see also note 2 on p. 128, below.

radically different things.[1] There is little doubt that the habit of confusing trends with laws, together with the intuitive observation of trends (such as technical progress), inspired the central doctrines of evolutionism and historicism—the doctrines of the inexorable laws of biological evolution and of the irreversible laws of motion of society. And the same confusions and intuitions also inspired Comte's doctrine of laws of succession—a doctrine which is still very influential.

The distinction, famous since Comte and Mill, between *laws of coexistence*, alleged to correspond to statics, and *laws of succession*, alleged to correspond to dynamics, can admittedly be interpreted in a reasonable way; i.e. as a distinction between laws that do not involve the concept of *time*, and laws into whose formulation *time* enters (for instance, laws that speak of velocities).[2] But this is not quite what Comte and his followers had in mind. When speaking of laws of succession, Comte thought of laws determining the succession of a 'dynamic' series of phenomena in the order in which we observe them. Now it is important to realize that 'dynamic' laws of succession, as Comte conceived them, do not exist. They certainly do not exist within dynamics. (I *mean* dynamics.) The closest approach to them in the field of natural science—and what he probably had in mind—are natural perio-

[1] A law, however, may assert that under certain circumstances (initial conditions) certain trends will be found; moreover, after a trend has been so explained, it is possible to formulate a law corresponding to the trend; see also note 1 on p. 129, below.

[2] It may be worth mentioning that equilibrium economics is undoubtedly *dynamic* (in the 'reasonable' as opposed to the 'Comtean' sense of this term), even though time does not occur in its equation. For this theory does not assert that the equilibrium is anywhere realized; it merely asserts that every disturbance (and disturbances occur all the time) is followed by an adjustment—by a 'movement' towards equilibrium. In physics, statics is the theory of equilibria and *not* of movements towards equilibrium; a static system *does not move*.

dicities like the seasons, the phases of the moon, the recurrence of eclipses, or perhaps the swings of a pendulum. But these periodicities, which in physics would be described as dynamical (though stationary), would be, in Comte's sense of these terms, 'static' rather than 'dynamic'; and in any case they can hardly be called laws (since they depend upon the special conditions prevailing in the solar system; see the next section). I will call them 'quasi-laws of succession'.

The crucial point is this: although we may assume that any actual succession of phenomena proceeds according to the laws of nature, it is important to realize that practically *no sequence of, say, three or more causally connected concrete events proceeds according to any single law of nature.* If the wind shakes a tree and Newton's apple falls to the ground, nobody will deny that these events can be described in terms of causal laws. But there is no single law, such as that of gravity, nor even a single definite set of laws, to describe the actual or concrete succession of causally connected events; apart from gravity, we should have to consider the laws explaining wind pressure; the jerking movements of the branch; the tension in the apple's stalk; the bruise suffered by the apple on impact; all of which is succeeded by chemical processes resulting from the bruise, etc. The idea that any concrete sequence or succession of events (apart from such examples as the movement of a pendulum or a solar system) can be described or explained by any one law, or by any one definite set of laws, is simply mistaken. There are neither laws of succession, nor laws of evolution.

Yet Comte and Mill did envisage their historical laws of succession as laws determining a sequence of historical events in the order of their actual occurrence. This may be seen from the manner in which Mill speaks of a method that 'consists in attempting, by a study and analysis of the general facts of history to discover . . . the law of progress; which law, once ascertained, must . . . enable us to predict future events, *just as after a few terms of an infinite series in algebra we are able to detect the principle of regularity in their formation, and to predict the rest of the series to any number of terms we please*'.[1] Mill himself is critical of this method; but his criticism (see the beginning of section 28) fully admits the possibility of finding laws of succession analogous to those of a mathematical sequence, even though he expressed doubts whether 'the order of succession . . . which history presents to us' may be sufficiently 'rigidly uniform' to be compared with a mathematical sequence.[2]

Now we have seen that there are no *laws* that determine the succession of such a 'dynamic' series of events.[3] On the other hand, there may be *trends* which are of this 'dynamic' character; for example, population increase. It may therefore be suspected that Mill had such trends in mind when he spoke of 'laws of succession'. And this suspicion is confirmed by Mill himself when he describes his historical law of progress as a *tendency*. Discussing this 'law', he expresses his 'belief . . . that the general *tendency* is, and will continue to be saving occasional and temporary exceptions, one of improvement—*a tendency towards a happier and better state*. This . . . is . . . a theorem of the science' (viz. of the social science). That Mill should seriously

[1] Mill, *Logic*, Book VI, ch. X, section 3. For Mill's theory of 'progressive effects' in general, see also Book III, ch. XV, section 2 f.

[2] Mill seems to overlook the fact that only the very simplest arithmetical and geometrical sequences are such that 'a few terms' suffice for detecting their 'principle'. It is easy to construct more complicated mathematical sequences in which thousands of terms would not suffice to discover their law of construction—*even if it is known that there is such a law*.

[3] For the nearest approach to such laws, see section 28, especially note 1 on p. 129.

discuss the question whether 'the phenomena of human society' revolve 'in an orbit' or whether they move, progressively, in 'a trajectory' [1] is in keeping with this fundamental confusion between laws and trends, as well as with the holistic idea that society can 'move' as a whole—say, like a planet.

In order to avoid misunderstandings, I wish to make it clear that I believe that both Comte and Mill have made great contributions to the philosophy and methodology of science: I am thinking, especially, of Comte's emphasis on laws and scientific prediction, of his criticism of an essentialist theory of causality; and of his and Mill's doctrine of the unity of scientific method. Yet their doctrine of historical laws of succession is, I believe, little better than a collection of misapplied metaphors. [2]

---

[1] See Mill, *loc. cit.* Mill distinguishes two senses of the word 'progress'; in the wider sense, it is opposed to cyclic change but does not imply improvement. (He discusses 'progressive change' in this sense more fully, *op. cit.*, Book III, ch. XV.) In the narrower sense, it implies improvement. He teaches that the persistence of progress in the wider sense is a question of *method* (I do not understand this point), and in the narrower sense a theorem of sociology.

[2] In many historicist and evolutionist writings it is often impossible to discover where metaphor ends and serious theory begins. (See for example the notes on pp. 111 and 114 of the present section.) And we must even face the possibility that some historicists may deny that there is a difference between metaphor and theory. Consider, for example, the following quotation from the psycho-analyst Dr. Karin Stephen: 'That the modern explanation which I have tried to put forward may still be no more than a metaphor I will concede . . . I do not think we need be ashamed . . . because scientific hypotheses are in fact all based on metaphor. What else is the wave theory of light . . . ?' (Cp. Waddington's *Science and Ethics*, p. 80; see also p. 76 on gravity.) If the method of science were still that of essentialism, i.e. the method of asking 'what *is* it?' (cp. section 10 above), and if the wave theory of light were the essentialist statement that light *is* a wave motion, then this remark would be justified. But as things are, it is one of the main differences between psycho-analysis and the wave theory of light that while the former is still largely essentialistic and metaphorical, the latter is not.

28   THE METHOD OF REDUCTION.
CAUSAL EXPLANATION. PREDICTION
AND PROPHECY.

My criticism of the doctrine of historical laws of succession is in one important respect still inconclusive. I
have tried to show that the 'directions' or 'tendencies'
which historicists discern in the succession of events
called history are not laws but, if anything, trends.
And I have pointed out why a trend, as opposed to a
law, must not in general be used as a basis for scientific
predictions.

But to this criticism, Mill and Comte—alone in this
respect among historicists, I believe—could still have
offered a rejoinder. Mill might perhaps have admitted
a certain amount of confusion between laws and
trends. But he could have reminded us that he himself
had criticized those who mistook a 'uniformity of
historical succession' for a true law of nature; that he
had been careful to emphasize that such a uniformity
could 'only be an empirical law' [1] (the term is somewhat misleading); and that it should not be considered
secure before it had been reduced, 'by the consilience
of deduction *a priori* with historical evidence', to the
status of a true law of nature. And he could have
reminded us that he had even laid down the 'impera-
tive rule never to introduce any generalization from
history into the social science unless sufficient grounds

---

[1] This and the next quotation are from Mill, *Logic*, Book VI, ch. X,
section 3. I consider the term 'empirical law' (used by Mill as a name for
a law of a low degree of generality) as very unfortunate because *all*
scientific laws are empirical: they are all accepted or rejected on the
basis of empirical evidence. (For Mill's 'empirical laws', see also *op. cit.*,
Book III, ch. VI, and Book VI, ch. V, section 1.) Mill's distinction has
been accepted by C. Menger who opposes 'exact laws' to 'empirical
laws'; see *The Collected Works*, vol. II, pp. 38 ff., and 259 ff.

can be pointed out for it',[1]—that is, by deducing it
from some true natural laws which can be established
independently. (The laws he had in mind were those
of 'human nature', i.e. psychology.) To this procedure of reducing historical or other generalizations
to some set of laws of higher generality, Mill gave the
name 'inverse deductive method', and he advocated it
as the only correct historical and sociological method.

I am ready to admit that there is some force in
this rejoinder. For should we succeed in reducing a
trend to a set of laws, then we should be justified in
using this trend, like a law, as a basis of predictions.
Such a reduction, or inverse deduction, would go a
long way towards bridging the gulf between laws and
trends. The force of this rejoinder is further brought
out by the fact that Mill's method of 'inverse deduction'
is a fair (although scrappy) description of a procedure
which is used not only in the social sciences but in
all sciences, and to an extent far beyond Mill's own
estimate.

In spite of these admissions I believe that my
criticism remains correct, and that the fundamental
historicist confusion of laws with trends is indefensible.
But in order to show this, a careful analysis is needed
of the method of reduction or inverse deduction.

Science, we may say, is confronted with problems,
at any moment of its development. It cannot start
with observations, or with the 'collection of data', as
some students of method believe. Before we can collect
data, our interest in *data of a certain kind* must be
aroused: the *problem* always comes first. The problem
in its turn may be suggested by practical needs, or
by scientific or pre-scientific beliefs which, for some
reason or other, appear to be in need of revision.

[1] See Mill, *op. cit.*, Book VI, ch. X, section 4. See also Comte, *Cours de philosophie positive*, IV, p. 335.

Now a scientific problem, as a rule, arises from the need for an *explanation*. Following Mill, we shall distinguish between two main cases: the explanation of an individual or singular specific event, and the explanation of some regularity or law. Mill puts it as follows: 'An individual fact is said to be explained by pointing out its cause, that is, by stating the law or laws . . . of which its production is an instance. Thus a conflagration is explained when it is proved to have arisen from a spark falling into a heap of combustibles; and in a similar manner, a law . . . is said to be explained when another law or laws are pointed out, of which that law itself is but a case and from which it could be deduced'.[1] The case of the explanation of a law is a case of 'inverse deduction', and therefore important in our context.

Mill's explanation of an explanation, or better of a causal explanation, is in the main quite acceptable. But for certain purposes it is not precise enough; and this lack of precision plays an important part in the issue we are here concerned with. I shall therefore re-state the matter, and point out where the differences between Mill's view and my own lie.

I suggest that to give a causal explanation of a certain *specific event* means deducing a statement describing this event from two kinds of premises: from some *universal laws*, and from some singular or specific statements which we may call the *specific initial conditions*. For example, we can say that we have given a causal explanation of the breaking of a certain thread if we find that this thread could carry a weight of only one pound, and that a weight of two pounds was put on it. If we analyse this causal explanation, then we find

[1] Mill, *op. cit.*, Book III, ch. XII, section 1. For the 'derivation' or 'inverse deduction' of what he calls 'empirical laws', see also *lib. cit.*, ch. XVI, section 2.

that two different constituents are involved. (*1*) Some hypotheses of the character of universal laws of nature; in this case, perhaps: 'For every thread of a given structure *s* (determined by its material, thickness, etc.) there is a characteristic weight *w* such that the thread will break if any weight exceeding *w* is suspended on it'; and 'For every thread of the structure s_1, the characteristic weight *w* equals one pound'. (*2*) Some specific (singular) statements—the initial conditions —pertaining to the particular event in question; in this case, we may have two statements: 'This is a thread of structure s_1', and 'The weight put on this thread was a weight of two pounds'. Thus we have two different constituents, two different kinds of statements which together yield a complete causal explanation: (*1*) *Universal statements of the character of natural laws*; and (*2*) *specific statements pertaining to the special case in question, called the 'initial conditions'*. Now from the universal laws (*1*) we can deduce, with the help of the initial conditions (*2*), the following specific statement (*3*): 'This thread will break'. This conclusion (*3*) we may also call a specific *prognosis*. The initial conditions (or more precisely, the situation described by them) are usually spoken of as the *cause* of the event in question, and the prognosis (or rather, the event described by the prognosis) as the effect; for example, we say that the putting of a weight of two pounds on a thread capable of carrying only one pound was the cause, and the breaking the effect.[1]

---

[1] This paragraph, containing the analysis of a causal explanation of a specific event, is a near-quotation from my *Logic of Scientific Discovery*, section 12. At present, I feel inclined to suggest a definition of '*cause*' on the basis of Tarski's semantics (which I did not know when that book was written), along the following lines: The (singular) event A is called a *cause* of the (singular) event B if and only if from a set of *true* universal statements (laws of nature) a material implication follows whose implicans designates A and whose implicate designates B. Similarly, we

Such a causal explanation will, of course, be scientifically acceptable only if the universal laws are well tested and corroborated, and if we have also some independent evidence in favour of the cause, i.e. of the initial conditions.

Before proceeding to analyse the causal explanation of regularities or laws, it may be remarked that several things emerge from our analysis of the explanation of singular events. One is that we can never speak of cause and effect in an absolute way, but must say that an event is a cause of another event—its effect—in relation to some universal law. However, these universal laws are very often so trivial (as in our example) that as a rule we take them for granted instead of making conscious use of them. A second point is that the use of a theory for *predicting* some specific event is just another aspect of its use for *explaining* such an event. And since we test a theory by comparing the events predicted with those actually observed, our analysis also shows how theories can be *tested*. Whether we use a theory for the purpose of explanation, of prediction, or of testing, depends upon our interest; it depends upon the question which statements we consider as given or unproblematic, and which statements we consider to stand in need of further criticism, and of testing. (See section 29.)

The causal explanation of a *regularity*, described by a universal law, is somewhat different from that of a singular event. At first sight, one might think that the case is analogous and that the law in question has to be deduced from (*1*) some more general laws, and (*2*)

could define the concept of a 'scientifically accepted cause'. For the semantic concept of designation, see Carnap, *Introduction to Semantics* (1942). It appears that the above definition could be improved by using what Carnap calls 'absolute concepts'.—For some historical remarks concerning the problem of cause, see note 7 to ch. 25 of my book, *The Open Society and Its Enemies*.

certain special conditions which correspond to the
initial conditions but which are *not* singular, and refer
to a certain *kind* of situation. This, however, is not
the case here, for the special conditions (*2*) must be
explicitly stated in the formulation of the law which
we wish to explain; for otherwise this law would
simply contradict (*1*). (For example, if with the help
of Newton's theory we wish to explain the law that all
planets move in ellipses, then we have to put first
explicitly in the formulation of this law the conditions
under which we can assert its validity, perhaps in the
form: *If* a number of planets, sufficiently spaced to
make their mutual attraction very small, move round
a very much heavier sun, *then* each moves approxi-
mately in an ellipse with the sun in the one focus.)
In other words, the formulation of the universal law
which we try to explain has to incorporate all the
conditions of its validity, since otherwise we cannot
assert it universally (or as Mill says, unconditionally).
Accordingly, the causal explanation of a regularity
consists in the deduction of a law (containing the conditions under which the regularity asserted holds) from
a set of more general laws which have been tested and
confirmed independently.

If we now compare our account of causal explanation with Mill's we see that there is no great difference as far as the reduction of laws to more general
laws is concerned, that is to say, in the causal explanation of regularities. But in Mill's discussion of the
causal explanation of *singular events*, there is no clear
distinction between (*1*) universal laws, and (*2*) specific
initial conditions. This is, largely, due to Mill's lack
of clarity in his use of the term 'cause' by which
he means sometimes singular events, and sometimes
universal laws. We shall now show how this affects
the explanation or reduction of trends.

That it is logically possible to reduce or explain trends cannot be doubted. Let us assume, for example, that we find that all planets progressively approach the sun. The solar system would then be a dynamic system in Comte's sense; it would have a development or a history, with a definite trend. The trend could easily be explained in Newtonian physics by the assumption (for which we might find independent evidence) that inter-planetary space is filled with some resisting matter—for example, a certain gas. This assumption would be a new specific initial condition which we would have to add to the usual initial conditions stating the positions and momenta of the planets at a certain time. As long as the new initial condition persists, we should have a systematic change or trend. Now if we further assume the change to be large, then it must have a very marked systematic influence on the biology and history of the various species on earth, including human history. This shows how we could, in principle, explain certain evolutionary and historical trends—even 'general trends', i.e. trends that persist throughout the development under consideration. It is obvious that these trends would be analogous to the quasi-laws of succession (seasonal periodicities, etc.) mentioned in the preceding section, with the difference that they would be 'dynamic'. They would, therefore, correspond, even more closely than these 'static' quasi-laws, to Comte's and Mill's vague idea of evolutionary or historical laws of succession. Now if we have reason to assume the persistence of the relevant initial conditions then, clearly, we can assume that these trends or 'dynamic quasi-laws' will persist, so that they may be used, like laws, as a basis for predictions.

There is little doubt that such *explained trends* (as we may call them), or trends which are on the verge of

being explained, play a considerable role in modern
evolutionary theory. Apart from a number of such
trends pertaining to the evolution of certain biological
forms such as shells and rhinoceroses, it appears that
a *general* trend towards an increasing number and an
increasing variety of biological forms spreading into
an increasing range of environmental conditions is
becoming explicable in terms of biological laws (together with initial conditions which make certain
assumptions regarding the terrestrial environment of
organisms and which, together with the laws, imply,
for example, the working of the important mechanism
called 'natural selection').[1]

All this may appear to tell against us, and indeed to
support Mill and historicism. But this is not the case.

[1] For a discussion of evolutionary trends, see J. Huxley, *Evolution*
(1942), ch. IX. Concerning Huxley's theory of Evolutionary Progress
(*op. cit.*, ch. X) it appears to me that all that can reasonably be asserted
is this: the general trend towards an increasing variety of forms, etc.,
leaves room for the statement that 'progress' (Huxley's definition is
discussed below) sometimes occurs, and sometimes not; that the evolutions of some forms is sometimes progressive, while that of most is not;
and that there is no general reason why we should expect that forms
will occur in the future which have made further progress. (Cp. Huxley's
contention—e.g. *op. cit.*, p. 571—that, if man were wiped out, further
progress is in the highest degree improbable. Although his arguments
do not convince me, they carry an implication with which I am inclined
to agree; namely, that biological progress is, as it were, something
accidental.) Concerning Huxley's *definition* of evolutionary progress as
increasing *all-round biological efficiency*, i.e. as increasing control over and
independence of the environment, I feel that he has indeed succeeded in
expressing adequately the intentions of many who have used this term.
Furthermore, the defining terms are not, I admit, anthropocentric; they
contain no valuation. And yet, to call an increase in efficiency or in
control 'progress' appears to me as expressing a valuation; it expresses
the belief that efficiency or control is good, and that the spread of life
and its further conquest of dead matter is desirable. But it is certainly
possible to adopt very different values. I do not think therefore that
Huxley's claim that he has given an 'objective definition' of evolutionary
progress, free from anthropomorphism and value judgments, is tenable.
(See *op. cit.*, p. 559; also p. 565, arguing against J. B. S. Haldane's view
that the idea of progress is anthropocentric.)

Explained trends do exist, but their persistence depends on the persistence of certain specific initial conditions (which in turn may sometimes be trends).

Now Mill and his fellow historicists *overlook the dependance of trends on initial conditions*. They operate with trends as if they were unconditional, like laws. Their confusion of laws with trends [1] makes them believe in trends which are unconditional (and therefore general); or, as we may say, in '*absolute trends*';[2] for example, in a general historical tendency towards progress—'a tendency towards a better and happier state'. And if they at all consider a 'reduction' of their tendencies to laws, they believe that these tendencies can be immediately derived from universal laws alone, such as the laws of psychology (or perhaps of dialectical materialism, etc.).

This, we may say, is the central mistake of historicism. *Its 'laws of development' turn out to be absolute trends*; trends which, like laws, do not depend on initial conditions, and which carry us irresistibly in a certain direction into the future. They are the basis of unconditional *prophecies*, as opposed to conditional scientific *predictions*.

But what about those who see that trends depend on conditions, and who try to find these conditions and to formulate them explicitly? My answer is that I have no quarrel with them. On the contrary: that trends occur cannot be doubted. Therefore we have the

[1] That in Mill's case it is this confusion which is mainly responsible for his belief in the existence of what I call 'absolute trends' can be seen by an analysis of his *Logic*, Book III, ch. XVI.

[2] There are some logical reasons for describing the belief in an absolute trend as unscientific or metaphysical (cp. note 1 on p. 115, above). Such a trend may be formulated by a non-specific or generalized existential statement ('There exists such and such a trend'), which we cannot test since no observation of deviation from the trend can disprove this statement; for we can always hope that, 'in the long run', deviations in the opposite direction will set matters right again.

difficult task of explaining them as well as we can, i.e. of determining as precisely as possible the conditions under which they persist. (See section 32.)[1]

The point is that these conditions are so easily over-looked. There is, for example, a trend towards an 'accumulation of means of production' (as Marx puts it). But we should hardly expect it to persist in a population which is rapidly decreasing; and such a decrease may in turn depend on extra-economic conditions, for example, on chance inventions, or conceivably on the direct physiological (perhaps bio-chemical) impact of an industrial environment. There are, indeed, countless possible conditions; and in order to be able to examine these possibilities in our search for the true conditions of a trend, we have all the time to try to imagine conditions under which the trend in question would disappear. But this is just what the historicist cannot do. He firmly believes in his favourite

[1] If we succeed in determining the complete or sufficient singular conditions c of a singular trend t, then we can formulate the universal law: 'Whenever there are conditions of the kind c there will be a trend of the kind t'. The idea of such a law is unobjectionable from the logical point of view; but it is very different from Comte's and Mill's idea of a law of succession which, like an absolute trend, or a law of a mathe-matical sequence, characterizes the general run of events. Besides, how could we determine that our conditions are sufficient? Or what amounts to the same thing: how could we *test* a law of the form indicated above? (We must not forget that we are here discussing position (*b*) of section 27, which involves the claim that the trend *can be tested*.) In order to test such a law we have to try hard to produce conditions under which it does not hold; to this end we must try to show that conditions of the kind c are insufficient, and that even in their pres-ence, a trend like t does not always occur. A method like this (it is sketched in section 32) would be unobjectionable. But it is inapplicable to the absolute trends of the historicist, since these are necessary and omnipresent concomitants of social life, and cannot be eliminated by any possible interference with social conditions. (We can see here again the 'metaphysical' character of the belief in trends which are not specific, such as general trends; the statements expressing such a belief cannot be tested; see also the foregoing note.)

trend, and conditions under which it would disappear are to him unthinkable. The poverty of historicism, we might say, is a poverty of imagination. The historicist continuously upbraids those who cannot imagine a change in their little worlds; yet it seems that the historicist is himself deficient in imagination, for he cannot imagine a change in the conditions of change.

29   THE UNITY OF METHOD

I suggested in the foregoing section that the deductive methods there analyzed are widely used and important —more so than Mill, for example, ever thought. This suggestion will now be further elaborated, in order to throw some light on the dispute between naturalism and anti-naturalism. In this section I am going to propose a doctrine of the unity of method; that is to say, the view that all theoretical or generalizing sciences make use of the same method, whether they are natural sciences or social sciences. (I postpone the discussion of the historical sciences until section 31.) At the same time, some of these doctrines of historicism which I have not yet sufficiently examined will be touched upon, such as the problems of Generalization; of Essentialism; of the role played by Intuitive Understanding; of the Inexactitude of Prediction; of Complexity; and of the application of Quantitative Methods.

I do not intend to assert that there are no differences whatever between the methods of the theoretical sciences of nature and of society; such differences clearly exist, even between the various natural sciences themselves, as well as between the various social sciences. (Compare, for example, the analysis of competitive markets and of Romance languages.) But I agree with Comte and Mill—and with many others, such as

C. Menger—that the methods in the two fields are
fundamentally the same (though the methods I have
in mind may differ from those they had in mind). The
methods always consist in offering deductive causal
explanations, and in testing them (by way of predictions). This has sometimes been called the hypothetical-
deductive method,[1] or more often the method of
hypothesis, for it does not achieve absolute certainty
for any of the scientific statements which it tests;
rather, these statements always retain the character of
tentative hypotheses, even though their character of
tentativeness may cease to be obvious after they have
passed a great number of severe tests.

Because of their tentative or provisional character,
hypotheses were considered, by most students of
method, as *provisional in the sense that they have ultimately
to be replaced by proved theories* (or at least by theories
which can be proved to be 'highly probable', in the
sense of some calculus of probabilities). I believe that
this view is mistaken and that it leads to a host of
entirely unnecessary difficulties. But this problem[2] is

[1] See V. Kraft, *Die Grundformen der wissenschaftlichen Methoden* (1925).

[2] See my *Logic of Scientific Discovery*, on which the present section is
based, especially the doctrine of tests by way of deduction ('deductivism')
and of the redundancy of any further 'induction', since theories always
retain their hypothetical character ('hypotheticism'), and the doctrine
that scientific tests are genuine attempts to falsify theories ('eliminationism'); see also the discussion of testability and falsifiability.

The opposition here pointed out, between *deductivism* and *inductivism*,
corresponds in some respects to the classical distinction between
rationalism and *empiricism*: Descartes was a deductivist, since he conceived
all sciences as deductive systems, while the English empiricists, from
Bacon on, all conceived the sciences as collecting observations from
which generalizations are obtained by induction.

But Descartes believed that the principles, the premises of the deductive systems, must be secure and self-evident—'clear and distinct'. They
are based upon the insight of reason. (They are synthetic and *a priori*
valid, in Kantian language.) As opposed to this, I conceive them as
tentative conjectures, or hypotheses.

These hypotheses, I contend, must be refutable in principle: it is of comparatively little moment here. What is important is to realize that in science we are always concerned with explanations, predictions, and tests, and that the method of testing hypotheses is always the same (see the foregoing section). From the hypothesis to be tested—for example, a universal law—together with some other statements which for this purpose are not considered as problematic—for example, some initial conditions—we deduce some prognosis. We then confront this prognosis, whenever possible, with the

here that I deviate from the two greatest modern deductivists, Henri Poincaré and Pierre Duhem.

Poincaré and Duhem both recognized the impossibility of conceiving the theories of physics as inductive generalizations. They realized that the observational measurements which form the alleged starting point for the generalizations are, on the contrary, *interpretations in the light of theories*. And they rejected not only inductivism, but also the rationalistic belief in synthetic *a priori* valid principles or axioms. Poincaré interpreted them as analytically true, as definitions; Duhem interpreted them as instruments (as did Cardinal Bellarmino and Bishop Berkeley), as means for the ordering of the experimental laws—the experimental laws which, he thought, were obtained by induction. Theories thus cannot contain either true or false information: they are nothing but instruments, since they can only be convenient or inconvenient, economical or uneconomical; supple and subtle, or else creaking and crude. (Thus, Duhem says, following Berkeley, there cannot be logical reasons why two or more theories which contradict one another should not all be accepted.) I fully agree with both these great authors in rejecting inductivism as well as the belief in the synthetic *a priori* validity of physical theories. But I cannot accept their view that it is impossible to submit theoretical systems to empirical tests. Some of them are testable, I think; that is, refutable in principle; and they are therefore synthetic (rather than analytic); *empirical* (rather than *a priori*); and *informative* (rather than purely instrumental). As to Duhem's famous criticism of crucial experiments, he only shows that crucial experiments can never *prove* or establish a theory; but he nowhere shows that crucial experiments cannot *refute* a theory. Admittedly, Duhem is right when he says that we can test only huge and complex theoretical systems rather than isolated hypotheses; but if we test two such systems which differ in one hypothesis only, and if we can design experiments which refute the first system while leaving the second very well corroborated, then we may be on reasonably safe ground if we attribute the failure of the first system to that hypothesis in which it differs from the other.

results of experimental or other observations. Agreement with them is taken as corroboration of the hypothesis, though not as final proof; clear disagreement is considered as refutation or falsification.

According to this analysis, there is no great difference between explanation, prediction and testing. The difference is not one of logical structure, but rather one of emphasis; it depends on *what we consider to be our problem* and what we do not so consider. If it is not our problem to find a prognosis, while we take it to be our problem to find the initial conditions or some of the universal laws (or both) from which we may deduce a *given* 'prognosis', then we are looking for an *explanation* (and the given 'prognosis' becomes our 'explicandum'). If we consider the laws and initial conditions as given (rather than as to be found) and use them merely for deducing the prognosis, in order to get thereby some new information, then we are trying to make a *prediction*. (This is a case in which we *apply* our scientific results.) And if we consider one of the premises, i.e. either a universal law or an initial condition, as problematic, and the prognosis as something to be compared with the results of experience, then we speak of a *test* of the problematic premise.

The result of tests is the *selection* of hypotheses which have stood up to tests, or the *elimination* of those hypotheses which have not stood up to them, and which are therefore rejected. It is important to realize the consequences of this view. They are these: all tests can be interpreted as attempts to weed out false theories— to find the weak points of a theory in order to reject it if it is falsified by the test. This view is sometimes considered paradoxical; our aim, it is said, is to establish theories, not to eliminate false ones. But just because it is our aim to establish theories as well as we can, we must test them as severely as we can; that is, we must try to find fault with them, we must try to falsify them. Only if we cannot falsify them in spite of our best efforts can we say that they have stood up to severe tests. This is the reason why the discovery of instances which confirm a theory means very little if we have not tried, and failed, to discover refutations. For if we are uncritical we shall always find what we want: we shall look for, and find, confirmations, and we shall look away from, and not see, whatever might be dangerous to our pet theories. In this way it is only too easy to obtain what appears to be overwhelming evidence in favour of a theory which, if approached critically, would have been refuted. In order to make the method of selection by elimination work, and to ensure that only the fittest theories survive, their struggle for life must be made severe for them.

This, in outline, is the method of all sciences which are backed by experience. But what about the method by which we *obtain* our theories or hypotheses? What about *inductive generalizations*, and the way in which we proceed from observation to theory? To this question (and to the doctrines discussed in section 1, so far as they have not been dealt with in section 26) I shall give two answers. (*a*) I do not believe that we ever make inductive generalizations in the sense that we start with observations and try to derive our theories from them. I believe that the prejudice that we proceed in this way is a kind of optical illusion, and that at no stage of scientific development do we begin without something in the nature of a theory, such as a hypo-thesis, or a prejudice, or a problem—often a techno-logical one—which in some way *guides* our observations, and helps us to select from the innumerable objects of observation those which may be of interest.[1] But if

[1] For a surprising example of the way in which even botanical observations are guided by theory (and in which they may be even

this is so, then the method of elimination—which is nothing but that of trial and error discussed in section 24—can always be applied. However, I do not think that it is necessary for our present discussion to insist upon this point. For we can say (*b*) that it is irrelevant from the point of view of science whether we have obtained our theories by jumping to unwarranted conclusions or merely by stumbling over them (that is, by 'intuition'), or else by some inductive procedure. The question, 'How did you first *find* your theory?' relates, as it were, to an entirely private matter, as opposed to the question, 'How did you *test* your theory?' which alone is scientifically relevant. And the method of testing described here is fertile; it leads to new observations, and to a mutual give and take between theory and observation.

Now all this, I believe, is not only true for the natural but also for the social sciences. And in the social sciences it is even more obvious than in the natural sciences that we cannot see and observe our objects before we have thought about them. For most of the objects of social science, if not all of them, are abstract objects; they are *theoretical* constructions. (Even 'the war' or 'the army' are abstract concepts, strange as this may sound to some. What is concrete is the many who are killed; or the men and women in uniform, etc.) These objects, these theoretical constructions used to interpret our experience, are the result of constructing certain *models* (especially of institutions), in order to explain certain experiences— a familiar theoretical method in the natural sciences (where we construct our models of atoms, molecules, solids, liquids, etc.). It is part of the method of explanation by way of reduction, or deduction from

influenced by prejudice), see O. Frankel, 'Cytology and Taxonomy of Hebe, etc.', in *Nature*, vol. 147 (1941), p. 117.

hypotheses. Very often we are unaware of the fact that we are operating with hypotheses or theories, and we therefore mistake our theoretical models for concrete things. This is a kind of mistake which is only too common.[1] The fact that models are often used in this way explains—and by so doing destroys—the doctrines of methodological essentialism (cp. section 10). It explains them, for the model is abstract or theoretical in character, and so we are liable to feel that we see it, either within or behind the changing observable events, as a kind of permanent ghost or essence. And it destroys them because the task of social theory is to construct and to analyse our sociological models carefully in descriptive or nominalist terms, that is to say, *in terms of individuals*, of their attitudes, expectations, relations, etc.—a postulate which may be called 'methodological individualism'.

The unity of the methods of the natural and social sciences may be illustrated and defended by an analysis of two passages from Professor Hayek's *Scientism and the Study of Society*.[2]

In the first of these passages, Professor Hayek writes:

'The physicist who wishes to understand the problems of the social sciences with the help of an analogy from his own field would have to imagine a world in which he knew by direct observation the inside of the atoms and had neither the possibility of making experiments with lumps of matter nor the opportunity to observe more than the interactions of a comparatively few atoms during a limited period. From his knowledge of the different kinds of atoms he could

[1] With this and the following paragraph, cp. F. A. von Hayek, 'Scientism and the Study of Society', parts I and II, *Economica*, vols. ix and x, where methodological collectivism is criticized and where methodological individualism is discussed in detail.

[2] For the two passages see *Economica*, vol. ix, p. 289 f. (italics mine).

build up models of all the various ways in which they could combine into larger units and make these models more and more closely reproduce all the features of the few instances in which he was able to observe more complex phenomena. But the laws of the macrocosm which he could derive from his knowledge of the microcosm would always remain "*deductive*"; they would, because of his limited knowledge of the data of the complex situation, scarcely ever enable him to predict the precise outcome of a particular situation; and he could never verify them by controlled experiment— although they might be *disproved* by the observation of events which according to his theory are impossible.'

I admit that the first sentence of this passage points to certain differences between social and physical science. But the rest of the passage, I believe, speaks for a complete *unity of method*. For if, as I do not doubt, this is a correct description of the method of social science, then it shows that it differs only from such interpretations of the method of natural science as we have already rejected. I have in mind, more especially, the 'inductivist' interpretation which holds that in the natural sciences we proceed systematically from observation to theory by some method of generalization, and that we can 'verify', or perhaps even prove, our theories by some method of induction. I have been advocating a very different view here—an interpretation of scientific method as deductive, hypothetical, selective by way of falsification, etc. And this description of the method of natural science agrees perfectly with Professor Hayek's description of the method of social science. (I have every reason to believe that my interpretation of the methods of science was not influenced by any knowledge of the methods of the social sciences; for when I developed it first, I had only the natural sciences in mind,[1] and I knew next to nothing about the social sciences.)

But even the differences alluded to in the first sentence of the quotation are not so great as may appear at first sight. It is undoubtedly true that we have a more direct knowledge of the 'inside of the human atom' than we have of physical atoms; but this knowledge is intuitive. In other words, we certainly use our knowledge of ourselves in order to frame *hypotheses* about some other people, or about all people. But these hypotheses must be tested, they must be submitted to the method of selection by elimination. (Intuition prevents some people from even imagining that anybody could possibly dislike chocolate.) The physicist, it is true, is not helped by such direct observation when he frames his hypotheses about atoms; nevertheless, he quite often uses some kind of sympathetic imagination or intuition which may easily make him feel that he is intimately acquainted with even the 'inside of the atoms'—with even their whims and prejudices. But this intuition is his private affair. Science is interested only in the hypotheses which his intuitions may have inspired, and then only if these are rich in consequences, and if they can be properly tested. (For the other difference mentioned in Professor Hayek's first sentence, i.e. the difficulty of conducting experiments, see section 24.)

These few remarks may also indicate the way in which the historicist doctrine expounded in section 8 should be criticized—that is to say, the doctrine that social science must use the method of intuitive understanding.

In the second passage, Professor Hayek, speaking of

---

[1] Cp. *Erkenntnis*, III, p. 426 f., and my *Logik der Forschung*, 1934, whose sub-title may be translated: 'On the Epistemology of the Natural Sciences'.

social phenomena, says: ' . . . our knowledge of the principle by which these phenomena are produced will rarely if ever enable us to predict the precise result of any *concrete* situation. While we can explain the principle on which certain phenomena are produced and can from this knowledge *exclude the possibility of certain results*, e.g. of certain events occurring together, our knowledge will in a sense be only negative, i.e. it will merely enable us to preclude certain results but not enable us to narrow the range of possibilities sufficiently so that only one remains'.

This passage, far from describing a situation peculiar to the social sciences, perfectly describes the character of natural laws which, indeed, can never do more than *exclude certain possibilities*. ('You cannot carry water in a sieve'; see section 20, above.) More especially the statement that we shall not, as a rule, be able 'to predict the precise result of any *concrete* situation' opens up the problem of the inexactitude of prediction (see section 5, above). I contend that precisely the same may be said of the concrete physical world. In general it is only by the use of artificial experimental isolation that we can predict physical events. (The solar system is an exceptional case—one of natural, not of artificial isolation; once its isolation is destroyed by the intrusion of a foreign body of sufficient size, all our forecasts are liable to break down.) We are very far from being able to predict, even in physics, the precise results of a *concrete* situation, such as a thunderstorm, or a fire.

A very brief remark may be added here on the problem of complexity (see section 4, above). There is no doubt that the analysis of any concrete social situation is made extremely difficult by its complexity. But the same holds for any concrete physical situation.[1] The

[1] A somewhat similar argument can be found in C. Menger, *Collected Works*, vol. II (1883 and 1933), pp. 259–60.

widely held prejudice that social situations are more complex than physical ones seems to arise from two sources. One of them is that we are liable to compare what should not be compared; I mean on the one hand concrete social situations and on the other hand artificially insulated experimental physical situations. (The latter might be compared, rather, with an artificially insulated social situation—such as a prison, or an experimental community.) The other source is the old belief that the description of a social situation should involve the mental and perhaps even physical states of everybody concerned (or perhaps that it should even be reducible to them). But this belief is not justified; it is much less justified even than the impossible demand that the description of a concrete chemical reaction should involve that of the atomic and sub-atomic states of all the elementary particles involved (although chemistry may indeed be reducible to physics). The belief also shows traces of the popular view that social entities such as institutions or associations are concrete natural entities such as crowds of men, rather than abstract models constructed to interpret certain selected abstract relations between individuals.

But in fact, there are good reasons, not only for the belief that social science is less complicated than physics, but also for the belief that concrete social situations are in general less complicated than concrete physical situations. For in most social situations, if not in all, there is an element of *rationality*. Admittedly, human beings hardly ever act quite rationally (i.e. as they would if they could make the optimal use of all available information for the attainment of whatever ends they may have), but they act, none the less, more or less rationally; and this makes it possible to construct comparatively simple models of their actions and inter-actions, and to use these models as approximations.

The last point seems to me, indeed, to indicate a considerable difference between the natural and the social sciences—perhaps *the most important difference in their methods*, since the other important differences, i.e. specific difficulties in conducting experiments (see end of section 24) and in applying quantitative methods (see below), are differences of degree rather than of kind. I refer to the possibility of adopting, in the social sciences, what may be called the method of logical or rational construction, or perhaps the 'zero method'.[1] By this I mean the method of constructing a model on the assumption of complete rationality (and perhaps also on the assumption of the possession of complete information) on the part of all the individuals concerned, and of estimating the deviation of the actual behaviour of people from the model behaviour, using the latter as a kind of zero co-ordinate.[2] An example of this method is the comparison between actual behaviour (under the influence of, say, traditional prejudice, etc.) and model behaviour to be expected on the basis of the 'pure logic of choice', as described by the equations of economics. Marschak's interesting 'Money Illusion', for example, may be interpreted in this way.[3] An attempt at applying the zero method to a different field may be found in P. Sargant Florence's

[1] See the 'null hypothesis' discussed in J. Marschak, 'Money Illusion and Demand Analysis', in *The Review of Economic Statistics*, vol. XXV, p. 40.—The method described here seems partly to coincide with what has been called by Professor Hayek, following C. Menger, the 'compositive' method.

[2] Even here it may be said, perhaps, that the use of rational or 'logical' models in the social sciences, or of the 'zero method', has some vague parallel in the natural sciences, especially in thermodynamics and in biology (the construction of mechanical models, and of physiological models of processes and of organs). (Cp. also the use of variational methods.)   [3] See J. Marschak, *op. cit.*

comparison between the 'logic of large-scale operation' in industry and the 'illogic of actual operation'.[1]

In passing I should like to mention that neither the principle of methodological individualism, nor that of the zero method of constructing rational models, implies in my opinion the adoption of a psychological method. On the contrary, I believe that these principles can be combined with the view [2] that the social sciences are comparatively independent of psychological assumptions, and that psychology can be treated, not as the basis of all social sciences, but as one social science among others.

In concluding this section, I have to mention what I consider to be the other main difference between the methods of some of the theoretical sciences of nature and of society. I mean the specific difficulties connected with the application of quantitative methods, and especially methods of measurement.[3] Some of these difficulties can be, and have been, overcome by the application of statistical methods, for example in demand analysis. And they *have to be overcome* if, for example, some of the equations of mathematical economics are to provide a basis even of merely qualitative applications; for without such measurement we should often not know whether or not some counteracting influences exceeded an effect calculated in merely qualitative terms. Thus merely qualitative considerations may well be deceptive at times; just as deceptive, to quote Professor Frisch, 'as to say that when a man tries to row a boat forward, the boat will be driven backward because of the pressure exerted by his feet'.[4] But it cannot be doubted that there are

[1] See P. Sargant Florence, *The Logic of Industrial Organisations (1933)*.
[2] This view is more fully developed in ch. 14 of my *Open Society*.
[3] These difficulties are discussed by Professor Hayek, *op. cit.*, p. 290 f.
[4] See *Econometrica*, I (1933), p. 1 f.

some fundamental difficulties here. In physics, for example, the parameters of our equations can, in principle, be reduced to a small number of natural constants—a reduction which has been successfully carried out in many important cases. This is not so in economics; here the parameters are themselves in the most important cases quickly changing variables.[1] This clearly reduces the significance, interpretability, and testability of our measurements.

30   THEORETICAL AND HISTORICAL SCIENCES

The thesis of the unity of scientific method, whose application to theoretical sciences I have just been defending, can be extended, with certain limitations, even to the field of the historical sciences. And this can be done without giving up the fundamental distinction between theoretical and historical sciences—for example, between sociology or economic theory or political theory on the one hand, and social, economic, and political history on the other—a distinction which has been so often and emphatically reaffirmed by the best historians. It is the distinction between the interest in universal laws and the interest in particular facts. I wish to defend the view, so often attacked as old-fashioned by historicists, that *history is characterized by its interest in actual, singular, or specific events, rather than in laws or generalizations.*

This view is perfectly compatible with the analysis of scientific method, and especially of causal explanation, given in the preceding sections. The situation is simply this: while the theoretical sciences are mainly interested in finding and testing universal laws, the

---

[1] See Lionel Robbins, in *Economica*, vol. V, especially p. 351.

historical sciences take all kinds of universal laws for granted and are mainly interested in finding and testing singular statements. For example, given a certain singular 'explicandum'—a singular event—they may look for singular initial conditions which (together with all kinds of universal laws which may be of little interest) explain that explicandum. Or they may *test* a given singular hypothesis by using it, along with other singular statements, as an initial condition, and by deducing from these initial conditions (again with the help of all kinds of universal laws of little interest) some new 'prognosis' which may describe an event which has happened in the distant past, and which can be confronted with the empirical evidence—perhaps with documents or inscriptions, etc.

In the sense of this analysis, *all* causal explanation of a singular event can be said to be historical in so far as the 'cause' is always described by singular initial conditions. And this agrees entirely with the popular idea that to explain a thing causally is to explain how and why it happened, that is to say, to tell its 'story'. But it is only in history that we are really interested in the causal explanation of a *singular* event. In the theoretical sciences, such causal explanations are mainly means to a different end—the testing of universal laws.

If these considerations are correct, then the burning interest in questions of origin shown by some evolutionists and historicists, who despise old-fashioned history and wish to reform it into a theoretical science, is somewhat misplaced. *Questions of origin are 'how and why' questions. They are comparatively unimportant theoretically* and usually have only a specific historical interest.

Against my analysis of historical explanation [1] it

[1] My analysis may be contrasted with that of Morton G. White, 'Historical Explanation' (*Mind*, N.S., vol. 52, pp. 212 ff.), who bases his analysis on my theory of causal explanation as reproduced in an article

may be argued that history *does* make use of universal laws contrary to the emphatic declaration of so many historians that history has no interest whatever in such laws. To this we may answer that a singular event is the cause of another singular event—which is its effect —only relative to some universal laws.[1] But these laws may be so trivial, so much part of our common knowledge, that we need not mention them and rarely notice them. If we say that the cause of the death of Giordano Bruno was being burnt at the stake, we do not need to mention the universal law that all living things die when exposed to intense heat. But such a law was tacitly assumed in our causal explanation.

Among the theories which the political historian presupposes are, of course, certain theories of sociology —the sociology of power, for example. But the historian uses even these theories, as a rule, without being aware of them. He uses them in the main not as universal laws which help him to test his specific hypotheses, but as implicit in his terminology. In speaking of governments, nations, armies, he uses, usually unconsciously, the 'models' provided by scientific or pre-scientific sociological analysis (see the foregoing section).

The historical sciences, it may be remarked, do not stand quite apart in their attitude towards universal laws. Whenever we encounter an actual application of science to a singular or specific problem we find a similar situation. The practical chemist, for example,

by C. G. Hempel. Nevertheless he reaches a very different result. Neglecting the historian's characteristic interest in singular events, he suggests that an explanation is 'historical' if it is characterized by the use of *sociological terms* (and theories).

[1] This has been seen by Max Weber. His remarks on p. 179 of his *Ges. Schr. zur Wissenschaftslehre* (1922) are the closest anticipation of which I know to the analysis offered here. But he is mistaken, I believe, when he suggests that the difference between theoretical and historical science lies in the degree of generality of the laws used.

who wishes to analyse a certain given compound—a piece of rock, say—hardly considers any universal law. Instead, he applies, possibly without much thought, certain routine techniques which, from the logical point of view, are tests of such *singular* hypotheses as 'this compound contains sulphur'. His interest is mainly a historical one—the description of one set of specific events, or of one individual physical body.

I believe that this analysis clarifies some well-known controversies between certain students of the method of history.[1] One historicist group asserts that history, which does not merely enumerate facts but attempts to present them in some kind of causal connection, must be interested in the formulation of historical laws, since causality means, fundamentally, determination by law. Another group, which also includes historicists, argues that even 'unique' events, events which occur only once and have nothing 'general' about them, may be the cause of other events, and that it is this kind of causation that history is interested in. We can now see that both groups are partly right and partly wrong. Universal law and specific events are together necessary for any causal explanation, but outside the theoretical sciences, universal laws usually arouse little interest.

This leads us to the question of the *uniqueness* of historical events. In so far as we are concerned with the historical explanation of typical events they must necessarily be treated as typical, as belonging to kinds or classes of events. For only then is the deductive method of causal explanation applicable. History, however, is interested not only in the explanation of specific events but also in the description of a specific event as such. One of its most important tasks is undoubtedly to describe interesting happenings in their

[1] See, for example, Weber, *op. cit.*, pp. 8 f., 44 f., 48, 215 ff., 233 ff.

peculiarity or uniqueness; that is to say, to include aspects which it does not attempt to explain causally, such as the 'accidental' concurrence of causally un-related events. These two tasks of history, the dis-entanglement of causal threads and the description of the 'accidental' manner in which these threads are interwoven, are both necessary, and they supplement each other; at one time an event may be considered as typical, i.e. from the standpoint of its causal explana-tion, and at another time as unique.

These considerations may be applied to the question of *novelty*, discussed in section 3. The distinction made there between 'novelty of arrangement' and 'intrinsic newness' corresponds to the present distinction be-tween the standpoint of causal explanation and that of the appreciation of the unique. So far as newness can be rationally analysed and predicted, it can never be 'intrinsic'. This dispels the historicist doctrine that social science should be applicable to the problem of predicting the emergence of intrinsically new events— a claim which may be said to rest ultimately on an insufficient analysis of prediction and of causal ex-planation.

31   SITUATIONAL LOGIC IN HISTORY. HISTORICAL INTERPRETATION

But is this all? Is there nothing whatever in the histori-cist demand for a reform of history—for a sociology which plays the role of a theoretical history, or a theory of historical development? (See sections 12 and 16.) Is there nothing whatever in the historicist idea of 'periods'; of the 'spirit' or 'style' of an age; of irresistible historical tendencies; of movements which captivate the minds of individuals and which surge on like a flood, driving, rather than being driven by, individual men? Nobody who has read, for example, the speculations of Tolstoy in *War and Peace*—historicist, no doubt, but stating his motives with candour—on the movement of the men of the West towards the East and the counter movement of the Russians towards the West,[1] can deny that historicism answers a real need. We have to satisfy this need by offering something better before we can seriously hope to get rid of historicism.

Tolstoy's historicism is a reaction against a method of writing history which implicitly accepts the truth of the principle of leadership; a method which attributes much—too much, if Tolstoy is right, as he undoubtedly is—to the great man, the leader. Tolstoy tries to show, successfully I think, the small influence of the actions and decisions of Napoleon, Alexander, Kutuzov, and the other great leaders of 1812, in the face of what may be called the logic of events. Tolstoy points out, rightly, the neglected but very great importance of the decisions and actions of the countless unknown individuals who fought the battles, who burned Moscow, and who invented the partisan method of fighting. But he believes that he can see some kind of historical determination in these events—fate, historical laws, or a plan. In his version of historicism, he combines both methodological individualism and collectivism; that is to say, he represents a highly typical combination—typical of his time, and, I am afraid, of our own—of democratic-individualist and collectivist-nationalistic elements.

This example may remind us that there are *some* sound elements in historicism; it is a reaction against the naïve method of interpreting political history merely as the story of great tyrants and great generals.

[1] This anticipates the problems recently laboured but not answered by Professor Toynbee.

148

Historicists rightly feel that there may be something better than this method. It is this feeling which makes their idea of 'spirits'—of an age, of a nation, of an army—so seductive.

Now I have not the slightest sympathy with these 'spirits'—neither with their idealistic prototype nor with their dialectical and materialistic incarnations—and I am in full sympathy with those who treat them with contempt. And yet I feel that they indicate, at least, the existence of a lacuna, of a place which it is the task of sociology to fill with something more sensible, such as an analysis of problems arising within a tradition. There is room for a more detailed analysis of the *logic of situations*. The best historians have often made use, more or less unconsciously, of this conception: Tolstoy, for example, when he describes how it was not decision but 'necessity' which made the Russian army yield Moscow without a fight and withdraw to places where it could find food. Beyond this *logic of the situation*, or perhaps as a part of it, we need something like an analysis of social movements. We need studies, based on methodological individualism, of the social institutions through which ideas may spread and captivate individuals, of the way in which new traditions may be created, and of the way in which traditions work and break down. In other words, our individualistic and institutionalist models of such collective entities as nations, or governments, or markets, will have to be supplemented by models of political situations as well as of social movements such as scientific and industrial progress. (A sketch of such an analysis of progress will be found in the next section.) These models may then be used by historians, partly like the other models, and partly for the purpose of explanation, along with the other universal laws they use. But even this would not be enough; it would still not satisfy all those real needs which historicism attempts to satisfy.

If we consider the historical sciences in the light of our comparison between them and the theoretical sciences, then we can see that their lack of interest in universal laws puts them in a difficult position. For in theoretical science laws act, among other things, as centres of interest to which observations are related, or as points of view from which observations are made. In history the universal laws, which for the most part are trivial and used unconsciously, cannot possibly fulfil this function. It must be taken over by something else. For undoubtedly there can be no history without a point of view; like the natural sciences, history must be *selective* unless it is to be choked by a flood of poor and unrelated material. The attempt to follow causal chains into the remote past would not help in the least, for every concrete effect with which we might start has a great number of different partial causes; that is to say, initial conditions are very complex, and most of them have little interest for us.

The only way out of this difficulty is, I believe, consciously to introduce a *preconceived selective point of view* into one's history; that is, to write *that history which interests us*. This does not mean that we may twist the facts until they fit into a framework of preconceived ideas, or that we may neglect the facts that do not fit.[1] On the contrary, all available evidence which has a bearing on our point of view should be considered carefully and objectively (in the sense of 'scientific objectivity', to be discussed in the next section). But it means that we need not worry about all those facts and aspects which have no bearing upon our point of view and which therefore do not interest us.

[1] For a criticism of the 'doctrine . . . that all historical knowledge is relative', see Hayek, in *Economica*, vol. X, pp. 55 ff.

Such selective approaches fulfil functions in the study of history which are in some ways analogous to those of theories in science. It is therefore understandable that they have often been taken for theories. And indeed, those rare ideas inherent in these approaches which can be formulated in the form of *testable hypotheses*, whether singular or universal, may well be treated as scientific hypotheses. But as a rule, these historical 'approaches' or 'points of view' *cannot be tested*. They cannot be refuted, and apparent confirmations are therefore of no value, even if they are as numerous as the stars in the sky. We shall call such a selective point of view or focus of historical interest, if it cannot be formulated as a testable hypothesis, a *historical interpretation*.

Historicism mistakes these interpretations for theories. This is one of its cardinal errors. It is possible, for example, to interpret 'history' as the history of class struggle, or of the struggle of races for supremacy, or as the history of religious ideas, or as the history of the struggle between the 'open' and the 'closed' society, or as the history of scientific and industrial progress. All these are more or less interesting points of view, and *as such* perfectly unobjectionable. But historicists do not present them as such; they do not see that there is necessarily a plurality of interpretations which are fundamentally on the same level of both, suggestiveness and arbitrariness (even though some of them may be distinguished by their *fertility*—a point of some importance). Instead, they present them as doctrines or theories, asserting that 'all history is the history of class struggle', etc. And if they actually find that their point of view is fertile, and that many facts can be ordered and interpreted in its light, then they mistake this for a confirmation, or even for a proof, of their doctrine.

On the other hand, the classical historians who

rightly oppose this procedure are liable to fall into a different error. Aiming at objectivity, they feel bound to avoid any selective point of view; but since this is impossible, they usually adopt points of view without being aware of them. This must defeat their efforts to be objective, for one cannot possibly be critical of one's own point of view, and conscious of its limitations, without being aware of it.

The way out of this dilemma, of course, is to be clear about the necessity of adopting a point of view; to state this point of view plainly, and always to remain conscious that it is one among many, and that even if it should amount to a theory, it may not be testable.

32 THE INSTITUTIONAL THEORY OF PROGRESS

In order to make our considerations less abstract, I shall try in this section to sketch, in very brief outline, a *theory of scientific and industrial progress*. I shall try to exemplify, in this way, the ideas developed in the last four sections; more especially the idea of situational logic, and of a methodical individualism which keeps clear of psychology. I choose the example of scientific and industrial progress because undoubtedly it was this phenomenon which inspired modern nineteenth-century historicism, and because I have previously discussed some of Mill's views on this subject.

Comte and Mill, it will be remembered, held that progress was an unconditional or absolute trend, which is *reducible to the laws of human nature*. 'A law of succession,' writes Comte, 'even when indicated with all possible authority by the method of historical observation, ought not to be finally admitted before it has been rationally reduced to the positive theory of human nature . . .' [1] He believes that the law of progress is deducible from a tendency in human individuals which impels them to perfect their nature more and more. In all this, Mill follows him completely, trying to reduce his law of progress to what he calls the 'progressiveness of the human mind' [2] whose first 'impelling force . . . is the desire of increased material comforts'. According to both Comte and Mill the unconditional or absolute character of this trend or quasi-law enables us to deduce from it the first steps or phases of history, without requiring any initial historical conditions or observations or data.[3] In principle, the whole course of history should be thus deducible; the only difficulty being, as Mill puts it, that 'so long a series . . ., each successive term being composed of an even greater number and variety of parts, could not possibly be computed by human faculties.' [4]

The weakness of this 'reduction' of Mill's seems obvious. Even if we should grant Mill's premises and deductions, it still would not follow that the social or historical effect will be significant. Progress might be rendered negligible, say, by losses due to an unmanageable natural environment. Besides, the premises are based on only one side of 'human nature' without considering other sides such as forgetfulness or indolence. Thus where we observe the precise opposite of the progress described by Mill, there we can equally well 'reduce' these observations to 'human nature'. (Is it not, indeed, one of the most popular devices of so-called historical theories to explain the decline and

---

[1] Comte, *Cours de philosophie positive*, IV, p. 335.
[2] Mill, *Logic*, Book VI, ch. X, section 3; the next quotation is from section 6 where the theory is worked out in more detail.
[3] Comte, *op. cit.*, IV, p. 345.
[4] Mill, *loc. cit.*, section 4.

fall of empires by such traits as idleness and a propensity to over-eat?) In fact we can conceive of very few events which could not be plausibly explained by an appeal to certain propensities of 'human nature'. But a method that can explain everything that might happen explains nothing.

If we wish to replace this surprisingly naïve theory by a more tenable one, we have to take two steps. First, we have to attempt to find *conditions* of progress, and to this end we must apply the principle set out in section 28: we must try to imagine *conditions under which progress would be arrested*. This immediately leads to the realization that a *psychological propensity alone* cannot be sufficient to explain progress, since conditions may be found on which it may depend. Thus we must, next, replace the theory of psychological propensities by something better; I suggest, by an *institutional* (and technological) analysis of the conditions of progress.

How could we arrest scientific and industrial progress? By closing down, or by controlling, laboratories for research, by suppressing or controlling scientific periodicals and other means of discussion, by suppressing scientific congresses and conferences, by suppressing Universities and other schools, by suppressing books, the printing press, writing, and, in the end, speaking. All these things which indeed might be suppressed (or controlled) are social institutions. Language is a social institution without which scientific progress is unthinkable, since without it there can be neither science nor a growing and progressive tradition. Writing is a social institution, and so are the organizations for printing and publishing and all the other institutional instruments of scientific method. Scientific method itself has social aspects. Science, and more especially scientific progress, are the results not of isolated efforts but of the *free competition of*

thought. For science needs ever more competition between hypotheses and ever more rigorous tests. And the
competing hypotheses need personal representation, as
it were: they need advocates, they need a jury, and
even a public. This personal representation must be
institutionally organized if we wish to ensure that it
works. And these institutions have to be paid for, and
protected by law. Ultimately, progress depends very
largely on political factors; on political institutions
that safeguard the freedom of thought: on democracy.

It is of some interest that what is usually called
'scientific objectivity' is based, to some extent, on social
institutions. The naïve view that scientific objectivity
rests on the mental or psychological attitude of the
individual scientist, on his training, care, and scientific
detachment, generates as a reaction the sceptical view
that scientists can never be objective. On this view
their lack of objectivity may be negligible in the
natural sciences where their passions are not excited,
but for the social sciences where social prejudices, class
bias, and personal interests are involved, it may be
fatal. This doctrine, developed in detail by the
so-called *'sociology of knowledge'* (see sections 6 and
26), entirely overlooks the social or institutional character of scientific knowledge, because it is based on the
naïve view that objectivity depends on the psychology
of the individual scientist. It overlooks the fact that
neither the dryness nor the remoteness of a topic of
natural science prevent partiality and self-interest
from interfering with the individual scientist's beliefs,
and that if we had to depend on his detachment,
science, even natural science, would be quite impossible. *What the 'sociology of knowledge' overlooks is just
the sociology of knowledge*—the social or public character
of science. It overlooks the fact that it is the public
character of science and of its institutions which imposes

a mental discipline upon the individual scientist, and which preserves the objectivity of science and its tradition of critically discussing new ideas.[1]

In this connection, I may perhaps touch upon another of the doctrines presented in section 6 (*Objectivity and Valuation*). There it was argued that, since scientific research in social problems must itself influence social life, it is impossible for the social scientist who is aware of this influence to retain the proper scientific attitude of disinterested objectivity. But there is nothing peculiar to social science in this situation. A physicist or a physical engineer is in the same position. Without being a social scientist he can realize that the invention of a new aircraft or rocket may have a tremendous influence on society.

I have just sketched some of the institutional conditions on whose realization scientific and industrial progress depends. Now it is important to realize that most of these conditions cannot be called necessary, and that all of them taken together are not sufficient.

The conditions are not necessary, since without these institutions (language perhaps excepted) scientific progress would not be strictly impossible. 'Progress', after all, *has* been made from the spoken to the written word, and even further (although this early development was perhaps not, properly speaking, *scientific* progress).

On the other hand, and this is more important, we must realize that with the best institutional organization in the world, scientific progress may one day stop. There may, for example, be an epidemic of mysticism. This is certainly possible, for since some intellectuals

[1] A fuller criticism of the so-called 'Sociology of Knowledge' will be found in ch. 23 of my *Open Society and Its Enemies*. The problem of scientific objectivity, and its dependence upon rational criticism and inter-subjective testability, is also discussed there in ch. 24, and, from a somewhat different point of view, in my *Logic of Scientific Discovery*.

do react to scientific progress (or to the demands of an open society) by withdrawing into mysticism, everyone *might* react in this way. Such a possibility may perhaps be counteracted by devising a further set of social institutions, such as educational institutions, to discourage uniformity of outlook and encourage diversity. Also, the idea of progress and its enthusiastic propagation may have some effect. But all this cannot make progress certain. For we cannot exclude the logical possibility, say, of a bacterium or virus that spreads a wish for Nirvana.

We thus find that even the best institutions can never be foolproof. As I have said before, 'Institutions are like fortresses. They must be well designed *and* properly manned'. But we can never make sure that the right man will be attracted by scientific research. Nor can we make sure that there will be men of imagination who have the knack of inventing new hypotheses. And ultimately, much depends on sheer luck, in these matters. For truth is *not manifest*, and it is a mistake to believe—as did Comte and Mill—that once the 'obstacles' (the allusion is to the Church) are removed, truth will be visible to all who genuinely want to see it.

I believe that the result of this analysis can be generalized. The human or personal factor will remain *the* irrational element in most, or all, institutional social theories. The opposite doctrine which teaches the reduction of social theories to psychology, in the same way as we try to reduce chemistry to physics, is, I believe, based on a misunderstanding. It arises from the false belief that this 'methodological psychologism' is a necessary corollary of a methodological individualism—of the quite unassailable doctrine that we must try to understand all collective phenomena as due to the actions, interactions, aims, hopes, and thoughts of individual men, and as due to traditions created and preserved by individual men. But we can be individualists without accepting psychologism. The 'zero method' of constructing rational models is *not* a psychological but rather a logical method.

In fact, psychology cannot be the basis of social science. First, because it is itself just one of the social sciences: 'human nature' varies considerably with the social institutions, and its study therefore presupposes an understanding of these institutions. Secondly, because the social sciences are largely concerned with the unintended consequences, or repercussions, of human actions. And 'unintended' in this context does not perhaps mean 'not *consciously* intended'; rather it characterizes repercussions which may violate *all* interests of the social agent, whether conscious or un-conscious: although some people may claim that a liking for mountains and solitude may be explained psychologically, the fact that, if too many people like the mountains, they cannot enjoy solitude there, is not a psychological fact; but this kind of problem is at the very root of social theory.

With this, we reach a result which contrasts start-lingly with the still fashionable method of Comte and Mill. Instead of reducing sociological considerations to the apparently firm basis of the psychology of human nature, we might say that the human factor is *the* ultimately uncertain and wayward element in social life and in all social institutions. Indeed this is the element which ultimately *cannot* be completely con-trolled by institutions (as Spinoza first saw [1]); for every attempt at controlling it completely must lead to tyranny; which means, to the omnipotence of the human factor—the whims of a few men, or even of one.

But is it not possible to control the human factor by *science*—the opposite of whim? No doubt, biology and

[1] See note 2 on p. 90, above.

psychology can solve, or will soon be able to solve, the
'problem of transforming man'. Yet those who attempt
to do this are bound to destroy the objectivity of
science, and so science itself, since these are both based
upon free competition of thought; that is, upon freedom. If the growth of reason is to continue, and human
rationality to survive, then the diversity of individuals
and their opinions, aims, and purposes must never be
interfered with (except in extreme cases where political
freedom is endangered). Even the emotionally satisfy-
ing appeal for a *common purpose*, however excellent, is an
appeal to abandon all rival moral opinions and the
cross-criticisms and arguments to which they give rise.
It is an appeal to abandon rational thought.

The evolutionist who demands the 'scientific' control of human nature does not realize how suicidal
this demand is. The mainspring of evolution and progress is the variety of the material which may become
subject to selection. So far as human evolution is
concerned it is the 'freedom to be odd and unlike one's
neighbour'—'to disagree with the majority, and go
one's own way'.[1] Holistic control, which must lead to
the equalization not of human rights but of human
minds, would mean the end of progress.

33   CONCLUSION. THE EMOTIONAL
APPEAL OF HISTORICISM

Historicism is a very old movement. Its oldest forms,
such as the doctrines of the life cycles of cities and
races, actually precede the primitive teleological view

---

[1] See Waddington (*The Scientific Attitude*, 1941, pp. 111 and 112), who
is prevented neither by his evolutionism nor by his scientific ethics from
denying that this freedom has any 'scientific value'. This passage is
criticized in Hayek's *The Road to Serfdom*, p. 143.

that there are hidden purposes [1] behind the apparently blind decrees of fate. Although this divination of hidden purposes is far removed from the scientific way of thinking it has left unmistakable traces upon even the most modern historicist theories. Every version of historicism expresses the feeling of being swept into the future by irresistible forces.

Modern historicists, however, seem to be unaware of the antiquity of their doctrine. They believe—and what else could their deification of modernism permit?—that their own brand of historicism is the latest and boldest achievement of the human mind, an achievement so staggeringly novel that only a few people are sufficiently advanced to grasp it. They believe, indeed, that it is they who have discovered the problem of change—one of the oldest problems of speculative metaphysics. Contrasting their 'dynamic' thinking with the 'static' thinking of all previous generations, they believe that their own advance has been made possible by the fact that we are now 'living in a revolution' which has so much accelerated the speed of our development that social change can be now directly experienced within a single lifetime. This story is, of course, sheer mythology. Important revolutions have occurred before our time, and since the days of Heraclitus change has been discovered over and over again. [2]

To present so venerable an idea as bold and revolu-

[1] The best immanent criticism of the teleological doctrine known to me (and one which adopts the religious point of view and especially the doctrine of creation) is contained in the last chapter of M. B. Foster's *The Political Philosophies of Plato and Hegel*.

[2] See my book *The Open Society and Its Enemies*, especially ch. 2 f.; also ch. 10, where it is argued that it is the loss of the unchanging world of a primitive closed society which is, in part, responsible for the strain of civilization, and for the ready acceptance of the false comforts of totalitarianism and of historicism.

tionary is, I think, to betray an unconscious conser-
vatism; and we who contemplate this great enthusiasm
for change may well wonder whether it is not only one
side of an ambivalent attitude, and whether there was
not some inner resistance, equally great, to be overcome. If so, this would explain the religious fervour
with which this antique and tottering philosophy is
proclaimed the latest and thus the greatest revelation
of science. May it not, after all, be the historicists who
are afraid of change? And is it not, perhaps, this fear of
change which makes them so utterly incapable of re-
acting rationally to criticism, and which makes others
so responsive to their teaching? It almost looks as if
historicists were trying to compensate themselves for
the loss of an unchanging world by clinging to the
faith that change can be foreseen because it is ruled
by an unchanging law.

Index

(A page number followed by 't' indicates a page on which a term is explained)

Index

education, 80, 90, 95, 157
eliminationism, 131-5
empiricism, 131-2
ENGELS, F., 72, 73
engineering, 65, 74, 83-4, 86, 92, 156; social —, 43t, 44, 47, 58, 64t, 73 (*see also* technology); piecemeal — —, 64t, 67, 68, 69, 86, 92-3; Utopian — —, 67t-70, 73, 74, 84
environment, 95-6, 100-2
essentialism, 27-28t, 31, 32, 33, 34, 40, 136; methodological —, 28t-29, 30, 33, 40, 119, 136
ethics, 54, 72, 73, 75, 88-9, 91-2, 115, 159 (*see also* values)
evolution, evolutionism, 51, 106, 107, 108, 109, 112, 115, 116, 127, 159
exactness, 13, 78
experiment, 98, 137, 139, 140 (*see also* observation); social —, 8-9, 43, 44, 83-8, 92, 96, 140; crucial —, 132; piecemeal experiments, examples of, 84
experimental conditions, 93-5, 97, 140
explanation, 20, 32, 35, 40, 122-3, 133; historical —, 143-6, 148-50, 153-4

falsification, 131-5, 137
FISHER, H. A. L., 109, 110
FLORENCE, P. SARGANT, 141, 142
FOSTER, M. B., 159
FRANKEL, O., 135
freedom and science, 90, 154-9
FRIEDRICH, C. J., 63
FRISCH, RAGNAR, 142
functionalism, 65

GALILEO GALILEI, 1, 60
GALTON, F., 107
generalizations, 6-8, 20, 41, 98, 101, 102, 109, 110-11, 120-1, 132, 134, 137 (*see also* inductivism)
geography, 95, 100
geology, 81
Gestalt, 76-8, 82-3
GINSBERG, M., 60
GOMPERZ, H., 77
governments, 31
group, group-spirit, 17-19, 23, 33, 149 (*see also* holism)

HALDANE, J. B. S., 127

HALLEY, EDMUND, 27
HAYEK, F. A. von, 56, 58, 60, 64, 77, 90, 105, 109, 111, 136, 137, 138, 139, 141, 142, 159
heaven on earth, 75
HEGEL, G. W. F., xi, 102, 159
HEMPEL, C. G., 145
HENRY VIII, 91
HERACLITUS, xi, 33, 160
HESIOD, 99
hierarchy of sciences, 12, 75, 157
historical prediction, *see* prediction
historical prophecy, *see* prophecy
historicism, historicists, 3t, 4t, 10, 30, 31, 32, 33, 34, 39, 40, 42, 45, 48, 49, 50-5, 57, 64, 70, 71, 73, 74, 80, 81, 84, 94, 95, 96, 99-100, 102, 105, 106, 112-13, 116, 119, 128, 129, 146, 147, 148, 151, 152, 159-61; refutation of historicism, ix-xi; historicist ethics, *see* ethics
historism, 17t
history, x, 9-10, 33, 39, 40, 45, 46, 81, 85, 95, 143-52; division of — into periods, 10-11, 41
holism, 17-19, 23, 66-7, 72, 74, 75, 76t-83, 85, 89, 114, 115, 159 (*see also* organic theory); — as a primitive approach, 75, 76
HUME, DAVID, 65
HUSSERL, EDMUND, 32
HUTT, W. H., 67
HUXLEY, JULIAN, 108, 127
HUXLEY, T. H., 55, 108
hypothesis, 45, 61, 65, 87, 98, 102-3, 106, 119, 122, 131, 132, 133, 136, 137, 138; historical —, 107, 109, 151, 155

imagination, 129-30
individualism, methodological individualism, 82, 136, 142, 148-9, 157
inductivism, 131-2, 134, 135, 137 (*see also* generalization)
inexactitude, 13-14, 38, 139
institutions, social, 18, 31, 32, 45, 46, 64, 65t, 66, 73, 135, 140, 149, 155, 157, 158; the human factor in —, 66, 69-70, 157, 158; institutional analysis, 154-7
instruments, 29, institutions as —, 65
interpretation of history, 50, 51, 52, 95, 150-2

Index

interventionism, 60–1
intuition, 135, 138 ; intuitive understanding, 20–3, 24, 31, 78, 79, 138
isolation, of factors, 8, 12, 94, 139
  (*see also* holism; abstraction; aspect)

KANT, I., 56
KEPLER, JOHANNES, 100, 101
knowledge, limitations of, x–xi, 64,
  77–8, 89–90
KRAFT, V., 131
KUTUZOV, M. I., 148

language, 29, 65, 154, 156
laws, 45, 61, 62, 63, 64, 102–3, 108–9,
  115, 116, 122–4 (*see also* hypothesis;
  explanation); causal —, 25–6,
  108, 117, 122–4; historical —, 3, 5,
  6, 26, 36, 41, 45, 51, 72, 107, 118,
  120, 146; — — of evolution and
  succession, 106, 108, 115, 116, 117,
  118, 119, 126, 128, 129, 152;
  natural —, 5, 25, 35–6, 61, 62,
  100–1, 102; sociological —, 6–7, 26,
  41, 45, 46, 51, 61–2, 99, 116 (list of
  examples of, 62); — — applied to
  historical study, 145; technological
  form of —, 61–3
liberalism, 66–7
LIPPMANN, W., 67
Logic of Scientific Discovery, xi, 61, 87,
  103, 107, 111, 115, 123, 131, 38
LUTHER, MARTIN, 91

MACHIAVELLI, NICCOLO, 91, 110
MALINOWSKI, B., 65
MANNHEIM, K., 67, 70, 75, 78, 79, 80,
  81, 99, 101, 102
MARSCHAK, J., 141
MARX, KARL, Marxism, xi, 49, 51,
  71, 72, 73, 84, 102, 129
mathematics, 24–5, 57, 118; mathematical economics, 57, 60 (note),
  141, 142
MENGER, CARL, 131, 139, 141
metaphor, 113–14, 119
metaphysical, metaphysics, 27, 30,
  59, 106, 115, 128, 129
meteorology, 43, 44, 73
method, methodology, 27, 54, 57, 69,
  70, 87–90, 98, 103, 119, 121–4, 131,
  137; practical usefulness of —, 57;

historical —, 71, 81, 85; holistic —,
  78–9, 84; political —, 88; sociological —, 1–2, 18–19, 20, 46, 75, 87,
  97, 119, 121; social aspects of —,
  90, 154–5 (*see also* anti-naturalism;
  essentialism; generalizations; hypothesis; inductivism; nominalism;
  objectivity; prediction, pro-naturalism; rationality; science; test)
MILL, J. S., 1, 61, 71, 72, 73, 85, 101,
  106, 116, 117, 118, 119, 120, 121,
  122, 125, 126, 127, 128, 129, 130,
  152, 153, 157, 158
models, 87, 135, 136, 137, 140, 141,
  145, 149
modernism, 54, 160
morals, *see* ethics; modernism
music, 77
mysticism, 78, 156

NAPOLEON, 148
navigation, 86
NEURATH, O., 103
NEWTON, ISAAK, 1, 36, 60, 101, 115,
  117, 125; *see* also economics
nominalism, 27t, 28; methodological
  —, 29t, 30
novelty, 9–11, 19, 23, 48, 146–7 (*see
  also* uniqueness)

objectivity, 15t–16, 152, 155–6, 158–9
observations, 35, 38–9, 43, 85–6,
  97–8, 121, 134, 150
Oedipus effect, 13t, 15–16
Open Society, The, xi, 54, 63, 73,
  124, 142, 160
optimism, 50, 52, 53, 54, 73
organic theory of society, 9, 19, 23,
  72–3, 81, 83, 110 (*see also* holism).

paleontology, 106
PASTEUR, LOUIS, 1, 60
PAULI, W., 82
perfectionism, 75
personality, 18, 33, 80
pessimism, 73
philosopher-king, 47
physics, x, 1, 5, 10, 14, 18–19, 20,
  24–6, 29, 31, 35, 39, 40, 43, 61, 63,
  82, 93, 95, 96, 97, 102–3, 112, 113,
  115, 116, 117, 119, 125, 126, 132,
  141, 143

164

Index

planning, 45, 48, 49, 50, 64, 66; improvised or unplanned —, 68-9; Utopian or large-scale or holistic or collectivist —, 70, 73, 75, 80, 81, 84, 89, 90, 91, 92; the benevolent planning authority, 91, 92

PLATO, ix, 1, 27, 28, 31, 55, 62, 73, 75, 110, 111, 159

POINCARÉ, HENRI, 132

point of view, 151-2

POLANYI, M., 55

politics, 30, 42, 57, 62, 63, 72, 87, 88, 90, 155; scientific —, 88

power, 62-3, 66, 90, 92, 110, 145

prediction, 12, 35-6, 37, 42, 43, 121, 124, 132, 133; prophetic *vs.* technological —, 43-4, 46; historical —, 3, 39, 40; short term —, 38, 44; long-term or large-scale —, 36-7, 42, 44, 113; — in social science, 15, 35, 37; — in astronomy, 36-7; — in meteorology, 43

problems, 121, 133, 134; selection of —, 55-7, 59, 121; public character of —, 59;—theoretical, prior to experiments, 98

prognosis, 123, 132, 133

progress, progressivism, 54, 72, 108, 110, 118, 119t, 127, 128, 152-3, 157; scientific —, 90, 103, 154, 156, 159

pro-naturalism, 2t, 3, 7, 29, 51, 52-3, 60, 105-6, 112-15

propaganda, 90, 157

prophecy, historical, 12-13, 43-4, 50, 113, 120, 128; — *vs.* technological prediction, *see* prediction

psychologism, 152, 154, 155, 157, 158

psychology, 1, 12, 14, 76-8, 82, 119, 121; — as a social science, 142, 158

PYTHAGORAS, 63, 114

quantitative method, 24-6, 142

rational action, rationality, 65, 140, 141, 157 (*see also* situational logic)

RAVEN, CHARLES E., 106

reduction, 121t, 125, 128, 135, 152-3, 157.

reforms, 66, 67, 68

religion, 106, 107, 156, 161

Republic, 62, 110

revolution, 47, 62, 160; Plato's law of revolutions, 62

ROBBINS, LIONEL, 143

Robinson Crusoe, 8, 84

RUSSELL, BERTRAND, 66

SCHMITT, C., 79

science, 56, 79, 138; theoretical or generalizing —, 55-7, 135; applied —, 42-3, 56, 57, 133, 146-7; social —, see social science; historical —, 143-7, 150; public character of —, 155-6, 158

'scientism', 60t, 63, 105t, 106, 112, 114

semantics, 124-5; A. Tarski's, 123

similarity, 93-4, 106

situation, 5, 11, 21-2, 63, 95, 100

situational logic, 149f. f. (*see also* rationality)

social contract, 65

social institutions, *see* institutions

socialism, 84

social sciences, sociology, 31, 33, 35, 48, 56, 58, 61, 135, 142, 158; backwardness of —, 1-3, 56; method of —, *see* method; task of —, 30, 35, 38, 42, 44, 45, 53, 56, 57, 59, 106, 136; technological —, 46, 48

social structure, 18-19, 23, 45, 46

social systems, 107, 113, 115

'society as a whole', 67-70, 71, 74, 75, 79, 81, 84, 88, 113, 114, 119

sociological laws, *see* laws

sociology of knowledge, 17t, 99, 155

SOCRATES, 67

SPENCER, H., 72, 73

SPENGLER, O., 110

SPINOZA, B. de, 90, 158

STALIN, JOSEPH, 91

statics, 39, 73, 112-13, 116, 126

statistics, 38, 57, 115; statistical methods in economics, 57

status quo, 62

STEPHEN, K., 119

taboo, 99

TARSKI, ALFRED, 123

TAWNEY, R. H., 91

technological approach, 60-1, 71-2

technological form of laws, 61-3, 66, 139

165